8 STEPS TO SIDE CHARACTERS

HOW TO CRAFT SUPPORTING ROLES WITH INTENTION, PURPOSE, AND POWER

SACHA BLACK

CONTENTS

For every writer ever marginalized for being weird, strange or unusual. You're not a side character.
You're a fucking hero.
This one's for you.

FUCK THE RULES

Where we pontificate about inevitability, break, burn, and banish the rules to the fuckit bucket, and discover why your imagination should be a rebel.

Of all the books I've written, this one was perhaps the most inevitable. Once you've spent time chiseling out your heroes into sculpted muscle-shaped weapons, and you've spent *equal* time crafting the ultimate villain—and yes, equal is italicized for a reason: bad guys deserve, demand, and require as much time spent on their creation as your heroes do—where else is there to go except your devious little minions?

Next in line are your friends and allies, mentors and mischief-makers, all the characters that make up supporting roles.

See, every time I write a book on characters, I impress the importance of developing that particular type of character. Villains are vital to conflict and storytelling but heroes are the lens through which your story is told... but what about side characters? It will come as no surprise to you that side characters are... you guessed it, super important. These pesky players need your attention because they are the pillars that prop up your protagonists.

Too often, writers slap a few side characters into their novel like they're nothing more than jam in a peanut butter and jelly sandwich. Tut, tut. That's not how these pillar-pumpkins should be treated. We need to paint them with as much skill and dedication as we've sculpted our muscled heroes and deadly demons.

To be clear, while this book will provide a raft of tips and tricks for helping you improve your characters and characterization overall, I focus predominantly on side characters. For the sake of simplicity, I'll mostly refer to "side characters" but insert whichever phrase is most relevant, be that supporting roles, minor players, sub characters, or any other name that tickles your nips.

Let us dwell on rules for a moment...

Rules are darling little things shaped like teddy bears and treacle and baby bunny rabbits...

Teddy bears are for kids.

I don't like treacle.

And baby bunny rabbits...?

Well, my cat eats them for a tasty weekend snack—*apologies to the baby bunny conservation society, no offense was meant in the writing of that sentence.*

Why are we talking about treacle and bunnies when we're learning about characters? Come now, my sinful wordsmiths, you know me well enough by now (and if you don't you will shortly); we need at least a brief chapter of hyperbole before I give you the good stuff. The tidbits and tactics for delightful character creation are coming, *I promise.*

But first, where was I? Ah yes, the rules.

Rules are shaped like cuteness and fluff, but really, they're demonic restraints sent from the literary under-gods. They are the enemy of muses, fledgling writers, and seasoned pros. A rule's sole goal is to thwart your book-writing shenanigans and constrain your imagination. Oh, and I do mean "writing rules." I'm not talking about the legal ones like "thou shall not murder, thieve or harm." I happen to agree with those ones. Those ones keep the assholes in line. Don't be an asshole—they're full of shit rather than words.

I like to start my craft books discussing the merits of rules in writing because, well, there are many, and mostly they're all bullshit. Unfortunately for us creatives, bullshit seems to spread quicker than viruses.

Here's the thing, for every teacher who ever told you to "show don't tell," I can show you a dozen ways "telling" can be effective and pull out a dozen random books all with moments of telling sprinkled liberally over their pages.

There are Oxford comma preachers, tutors who hate adverbs, ones who say even purposeful repetition is bad and yet more who will say you can never filter as an author.

Listen to Sacha.

It's all bullshit.

Prose is art.

Art is subjective.

For every reader who adores clean prose, there will be a plethora of others who much prefer indulgent, rich prose. That's why we have R&B, Dubstep, and acoustic music. Everyone likes their own shade of sound. And readers, the darlings, like their own shade of sentence.

But... as much as I like to break a lot of rules, it would be remiss of me not to admit that these supposed rules do come from somewhere. Many of them were supposed to be guidelines, suggestions to help you say exactly what you want to say —rather than what you think you said—which actually came out more like the strangled afterbirth of a hangover. Over time, these "supposed" rules became cardinal law. Someone dipped their fingers in the ink well and played God with us lowly word-smiths. That was a booboo.

Whatever your word fetishes are, it's okay. You can rub adverbs over your word-nipples if you like. I mean, I don't want to, but if that's your thing, you do you, baby.

Any rule can be broken if you're skilled enough. When I say "must this" and "must that," you don't have to agree with me. I'm not here to argue with you. Just to present some principles and techniques you could use to help you craft solid side characters and minions for your stories.

What I do suggest, though, is that you spend some time both reading and researching in your genre. See, while I don't care much for *rules,* there are many readers who do appreciate it if you give them the tropes of their genres. A romance reader is gon' be pissed if you don't give them a happily ever after. Epic fantasy readers have a penchant for the *epic,* crime books... well, they need a dead body—some "rules" are rather important.

I'm not going to detail the construction of supporting roles for specific genre tropes, it would take a book the size of an encyclopedia and it's your job to know your genre.

Consider this your first piece of homework, if you can't reel off at least five tropes or expectations in terms of style, length, tone for your genre without having to scan your bookshelf, you don't know your genre well enough. Take your word-booty to your local independent bookstore and buy some books. Better still, help your friendly neighborhood indie author and order a couple of their books from your genre too.

Done that?

Good.

Now, I always like to caveat my books. Here's why you should put this book down:

- **You've come for advice about heroes and villains.** Erm... I've already written those books. If you're after specifics for improving your protagonists or antagonists, then I have two books that will help you:

13 Steps to Evil: How to Craft Superbad Villains
10 Steps to Hero: How to Craft a Kickass Protagonist
You should note though, there will be some deliciously helpful principles in this book for developing any character—heroes and villains included—but we are, in the main, focusing on those devious little side characters.

- **You're not interested in developing your characters.** Did you miss the title of this book? With craft, characters, or writing in general, I do insist you push yourself outside your comfort zone—it's the only way to develop. If you don't want to do the dirty and aren't willing to look at where your writing needs to improve, then you're wasting your time reading this. Yes, I'm not pulling punches, I'll always give it to you straight. It's a theme. You should probably get used to it.
- **You don't like dark humor or swear words.** I have a hardened potty mouth—her name is Helga, and she's at least eight hundred and fifty-six (and a half). Which means she's old, has a twisted sense of humor, and enjoys making shit up. It is what it is. It's my burden to carry. Helga is a rather delightful shade of marmite—either you love her or hate her—I understand if you fall into the hate camp of marmite fuckery.

Examples in this Book

In this book I've used examples from works I've written as well as from popular books, TV, and film. Why? Because a significantly larger proportion of the population have watched TV and movies than read books. Which means if I use a movie example, it's *far* more likely to resonate with a larger portion of readers. That aside, movies do in ninety minutes what authors do in four hundred pages. Movies are books on steroids— they're concise and the good ones have cracking story structure. I know it's controversial, but Disney/Pixar films create an array of excellent examples of different storytelling devices. We can all learn something.

While I love using quotes and examples from "in real life" books and Hollywood, to deliver this book to you sometime during my lifetime, it's occasionally quicker to construct an example than it is to trawl through the thousands of books I've read looking for something specific. I encourage you to do your own research and find examples from your genre for whatever devilish delight we're talking about.

I've given spoiler warnings at the top of each "step"; I've been as comprehensive as I can be, which means some of the spoiler warnings are for referencing just the first line of the story, others are full breakdowns of the novel.

Right, then, I think we've debated rule bending and individualism enough.

Are you ready to push up your Shakespearian sleeves and dive into improving your side characters?

Excellent.

Let us begin.

STEP 1 WTF IS A SIDE CHARACTER?

1.0 WTF IS A SIDE CHARACTER?

Where we sprinkle a dash of side and add a dusting of cameos, sniff clarity like it's a drug, fight combatants, pat our corporately inclined managers on the head, discover a guy with "skillzzz," and remember Stan Lee.

∾

Spoiler warning for books: *The Sky Is Everywhere* by Jandy Nelson, *Peter Pan* by J.M Barrie, *To Kill a Mockingbird* by Harper Lee, *The Hunger Games* by Suzanne Collins, *The Glamourist Histories* by Mary Robinette Kowal, *Harry Potter and the Philosopher's Stone* by J.K. Rowling, *The Eye of the World* by Robert Jordan, *Hatchet* by Gary Paulsen, *Nevernight* by Jay Kristoff, *Roseblood* by A.G. Howard.

Spoiler warning for movies: *The Trial of the Incredible Hulk, Thor,* and *Captain America: The First Avenger. The Darkest Minds, Who Framed Roger Rabbit, Bill and Ted* or *Dumb and Dumber, The Addams Family, Toy Story, Toy Story 2, A Christmas Carol, Pulp Fiction, Star Wars, Mean Girls, Taken, Castaway, The Minority*

Report and *The Matrix.*

Spoiler warning for TV shows: *Star Trek.*

∾

What a Side Character Is Not

Creating characters can be somewhat of an enigmatic process. For a lot of writers, characters spring forth from that weird well. You know... the intangible, muse-like inspiration that no one can quite put a finger on. I remember the last time it happened to me. I was minding my own business, strolling through the park with my son when I passed a stray lamp post. Such was the strike of breathtaking, limb-shivering, vagina-tingling inspiration, that I promptly halted in the middle of the path and bent double. If you're anything like me, then these tingly lightning bolts will oscillate between sheer terror— because holy shit, the enormity of the idea you now need to write—and unadulterated pleasure at the magical character/plot/story theme that's just been bestowed upon you by the muse-Gods.

But before you howl at the moon and dance beneath the stars showering yourself in celebratory champagne, you have to acknowledge the elephant-sized character problem. While the muses kindly drop the raw carcass of a character in your lap, they are fickle fucks and rarely give you all the finesse and detail you need to flesh out said character into a fully formed plot. Oh no, we have to do the work.

If we spent our creative careers hanging around waiting for the muses to strike, it would be a very unproductive, quiet career with few books published and fewer fans reading them. Nay, the muse-Gods make us work for it. We must chisel and sculpt until our hands bleed, our characters have individual fine marble lashes, and our stories are filled with heart-wrenching emotions.

In reality, creating characters is somewhat of a dual process, a strike of inspiration be that from the soul of your story itself, from a mood board, a book or TV show you've read or watched, or, lest we forget the pustules masquerading as human coworkers in the office with horrific eating habits—I mean it would be rude not to work them into your story just so you can poison their potato salad.

Let's look at the problem the muses leave us with. That initial bolt of lightning is only one tiny morsel of a character. Much as the irritating coworker's eating habits would be fun to destroy, eating habits do not make a full-bodied character with depth and life. These "slices" of inspiration provide just that—a teeny bite out of the character cake. It's not enough to sustain an entire novel. Your work is not done. This is only the start of character creation.

Characters who stay as they were conceptualized are card-board cutouts. Stories—whether you believe it or not—are kooky sentient magic. They evolve and change and if you don't take your character deeper than your initial idea, they'll end up as nothing more than a fleeting and entirely forgettable plot device.

Why am I saying that? Because characters need depth and they have to change during your story, those that don't are woefully boring to read—they say the same things, learn nothing, and don't grow.

Bleugh.

Of course, the clever dicks out there will be shouting about those character rebels who are exceptions to that rule.

Well okay then, let's 'ave at 'em...

Characters in episodic series, where each book contains a single open-and-shut case be it magical or crime; think Patricia Cornwell's *Kay Scarpetta* series or Jim Butcher's *Dresden Files* tend to have characters that don't change. But that's the appeal of those guys. However, you'll find over the length of the series those characters do change in some way whether it's growth, decision making, learning something new, or developing a private life. And if they don't do any of those, well then, my suspicion is they're changing the environment around them instead.

No more shall we allow our supporting characters to be mere add-ons. From this day forth, we shall take out our clay cutters, ribs and ribbons, our wire tools and brushes, our keyboards and hacksaws, our drill bits and...

Ahem.

That is to say, we're going to craft characters the right way.

Right, what, exactly, are side characters?

Actually, before we cover that, let's start at the beginning... with story.

What Is "Story," This Strange Thing in Which Our Characters Reside?

For anyone who's read my other books, you'll know I talk about how story is change. It's the emotional change one character experiences. But if we put character aside for a second and allow ourselves a little pontification, we can get to the meat of what story is.

Is story not an idea? Specifically, the idea of how change can play out? How change can affect and impact a character and their relationships? I heard Lisa Cron once say that all stories are really about the cost of human connection. I'm not sure I've ever heard a truer truth. Think about it. Let's take three random stories:

- *Peter Pan* — the cost of loving someone you can't keep

- *Taken* (movie) — the cost of loving your child
- *The Hunger Games* — the cost of wanting to protect your family

Now of course, when you look at each of these stories at the surface level, that's not at all how they come across. *The Hunger Games* is a dystopian story about the horrors of the corruption of power and hardcore fighting to the death. Peter Pan is about fairies and pirates, imagination and the embodiment of good and evil. *Taken* is a thrill ride of action, fighting, and moody phone calls with a guy who has a set of *skillzzz*.

And yet, each story is much more than that.

Taken embodies that deep, desperate love for a child. The idea that you'd go to the ends of the earth to protect your children. Isn't that the crux of it? Your characters are the embodiment of your book's soul—the idea buried inside the story... *the theme*. Your characters are walking metaphors and emotional sucker punches to the gut. All of which embody the intangible idea (theme) buried between the ink in your book's pages.

Without character there is no story to tell. Characters are story, they are theme, and action and emotion. They are the mechanism through which your story, your change, and your theme is conveyed.

That's real swell and all, Sacha, but could you explain what a side character is already?

Patience my dear, I'm getting there.

First, we discuss what they are not.

"Out of Scope"

If you've hung around me for any length of time, you'll know I'm rather scarred from my time in the corporate hellscape that was working for "The Man." However, one rather handy spill-over I've kept is the notion of defining what's in and out of scope. When we used to start a new corporate project, we'd define both what we were going to do as well as what we weren't. In other words, what was out of scope. This was particularly helpful for us lowly minions because every time a senior manager tried to nudge the project in another direction we'd turn around and pat the indecisive munchkin on the head and in our most humble, passive aggressive voice, say, "I don't think so, boss."

It was a handy tool back then, therefore let us use it again now and start with what a side character is not. Obviously, a side character is not the protagonist.

According to dictionary.com a protagonist is an:

> "'actor who plays the first part,' literally, 'first combatant,' equivalent to *prôt(os)* 'first' + *agōnistés* 'one who contends for a prize, combatant, actor'"

Which means your average side character—while they could well be combative in nature—is not the sacrificial lamb who flings themselves into battle *first*. That privilege is reserved for the protagonist. Whatever side characters are, they don't take center stage, or bellow "CHARGE" from the pit of their lungs, they don't take the lead, they don't make the final blow, and they don't get to shower themselves in golden glory. While they are integral to the story, they are not *who* the story is about —no matter how hard they tantrum or try to steal the limelight.

Many writers do class the villain or antagonist as a side character, and I agree, given they're not the protagonist. However, because I've already written a book on villains, I don't want to dive into any specifics about them here and risk repeating myself. But, yes, I do class villains and antagonists as side characters "of sorts" but I won't be focusing on them in this book specifically; that said, all the tricks here can be applied to their creation as much as they can to the other types of side character.

WTF Are Side Characters?

We've established what your side characters are not. Let's try and narrow the definition of what they are.

We writers like words. They're our thang. We toss them around until "people" give us that wide-eyed stare and we know without doubt it's time to step away from the thesaurus before we melt their brain. I suppose it's no different to an engineer vomiting engineering-geek all over us or a theoretical physicist talking about string theory. When we're in the throes of "our thang" we go hard and deep... how saucy.

We authors need to know the difference between heroes, villains, and side characters. Those are our words.

Here we are...

Side characters are the arteries in a protagonist-heart, they are new perspectives and viewpoints, conflict generators, and subplot fulfillers. When you get to the sticky innards of a story and its characters, all characters are the embodiment of the idea behind your story. In other words, your theme.

They manage this by drawing theme into reality through engaging in conversation, action, and obstacles all based on that theme. Characters are a metaphor that make the idea and concept of theme real to us. It is through the detail of character actions, emotions, and interactions that we come to understand what theme really means.

Look at it like this—if your book and theme were a math equation, the protagonist would be the solution. The antagonist would be the wrong answer and your side characters would be the workings out or alternative solutions you discarded along the way.

1.1 A FEW DEFINING TERMS

When it comes to story craft, there is a seething mass of jargon in the world. There are arcs and archetypes and then plain old types and lest we forget themes and plot points and dark nights... the list goes on.

One area we're going to rough and tumble in is the terminology around character. Shortly, we'll cover the difference between the various shades of side character: cameos, minor, and major characters. But before we do that, we should cover a few other angles on characters. Like any word, semantic-arguers will slap each other endlessly with the nuances. We don't have time for that, I'm just going to give you definitions based on how I personally see them and how I'll be referring to them in this book.

Character versus Characterization

A short, but no less important clarification. Character and characterization are often used interchangeably, hell, even I do it. But I probably shouldn't because while they sound the same, and while they're part and parcel of a whole, they are not, in fact, the same thing. Clarity is my drug of choice, thus, let us ensure we are crystal about the two:

Character is internal. It's the *who* of who a character is. It refers to the traits and whatever is at their core. Character is what you don't see, it's subtext and shadows, it's the foundations and pillars laid in a house—you know they're there supporting the house; you just can't see them.

Characterization is everything on the surface. It's the physical appearance of your character. It's the clothes they wear, the tone of their dialogue, the observable actions in a story. Characterization is the embodiment of character in a scene. It's what the reader sees and what shows them the "character" they can't see. Characterization and character affect and influence each other, they are osmotic in nature, they percolate between, through and around each other.

Character is focused inward. Characterization is mostly focused outward toward the reader. They are the yin and yang of characters.

Note: both character and characterization should be shown and not told, it is far more revealing and engaging for a reader to be shown than told these aspects.

The Reader

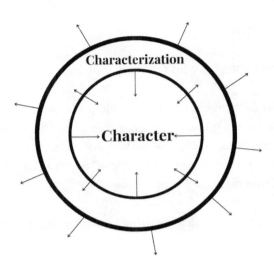

Character Role

Character roles are simply the role they play in the book. This "character role" phrase is simple until you bring in character archetypes which sound uncomfortably similar. They're not, but we'll cover that later. Think of character role as a job type. I'm sure if you've ever been employed by a business of any size, you'll have had a job role description, perhaps you even saw it as part of the application process. Well, it's the same thing in fiction with one small difference. There are only so many classic roles in fiction. I say classic because there's always room for rebels and rule breakers.

The classic roles are:

- Protagonist
- Antagonist
- Love Interest

- Deuteragonists*
- Foil

The Protagonist

The protagonist is who the story is about.

"In most (although not all) cases, the protagonist is the one who learns and grows and changes the most. They also take the biggest risks against the darkest evils and, despite those risks, they make the greatest sacrifices." Sacha Black, *10 Steps to Hero: How to Craft a Kickass Protagonist*

For an in-depth look at crafting a protagonist, I recommend my book *10 Steps to Hero*.

The Antagonist

While I draw a distinction between villain and antagonist, their role in a story is the same—to oppose the protagonist and get in their way. The difference is that:

An antagonist is a character or thing that opposes the protagonist (or hero). An antagonist does not have to be a villain.

A villain is an antagonist because they oppose the hero. But a villain also indicates some level of evil while an antagonist does not.

For an in-depth look at crafting an antagonist or villain, you can read my book *13 Steps to Evil: How to Craft Superbad Villains*.

Love Interest

I won't lie, this is definitely one of my favorite roles, not that

I'm soft and gooey on the inside, obviously... I'm dead on the inside.

ahem

The love interest does what it says on the tin. It's the person or object of the protagonist's desire. I've said person or object for a reason. In a buddy love movie like *Bill and Ted* or *Dumb and Dumber*, the "buddies" don't want to poke each other with their genitals, but they do *love* each other. Therefore, the buddy functions as the love interest in "role" terms.

Deuteragonists

A deuteragonist is essentially the second protagonist, the next most important character after villain and hero. A deuteragonist can flip flop their allegiances, either supporting or, in some stories, opposing the protagonist. In some stories, like heists or where the "friend" group is of key import, you can have a group of deuteragonists—Ron and Hermione in *Harry Potter*, for example. Dr. Watson from *Sherlock Holmes* is another example of a deuteragonist.

The classicists among us, will have noticed that I did not include confidant/e. This is because it's similar to a deuteragonist. A confidant/e is a key character the protagonist confides in. The difference, if we're being pedantic, is that a confidant/e doesn't have to be a secondary protagonist in the way a deuteragonist is. Plus, in its pure form it's lost traction in modern literature in favor of the mentor archetype, and thus, let's make shit simple and stick with deuteragonist or mentor.

Foil

A common misunderstanding is that the foil is the villain or antagonist. No, no, of course *they can be* one and the same. But they don't have to be. The foil is whichever character is the direct opposite to the protagonist. The character whose differences help to create the sharp clarity and relief of the protagonist's personality. In *Star Trek*, Mr. Spock is so wildly different to Captain Kirk that it helps to define both of their personalities better. Draco Malfoy in *Harry Potter* is another example, although here Malfoy also serves as a minor antagonist.

What Is an Archetype?

Archetypes are functions that your characters play in your story. I like to separate out the classic definition of "archetype" because archetypal characters are seen as that and that alone, whereas in modern literature, a character might be an archetype but it's rarely their sole purpose and function. Often these characters have mini subplots and arcs of their own and that is different to their function as an archetype.

"Think of it [archetypes] as character cosplay for story pace. If you forced a character to act as a mentor to the hero for the entire plot and only that, you're squeezing your character into such a tiny box you flatten them, literally and figuratively [...] Forcing your hero or another character to serve one purpose only is simplistic at best and, at worst, traitorous to your novel's potential." Sacha Black, *10 Steps to Hero: How to Craft a Kickass Character*.

Character Arc Type

Some characters have arcs and change dramatically through a story even if they themselves are not the protagonist. Other characters are stoically consistent—these are usually characterization types, more on this later—and others are somewhere in between. While purists may argue that these characters are all separate—and perhaps it's the rebel in me but—I believe they are often Venn diagrams of each other.

Static characters are sometimes also stock characters, symbolic characters are sometimes round characters. What these terms are not for, is making you think you must label each character as one thing and forever hold your peace. Far from it. I'm not going to chase you down the street waving hardbacks and whips because you have a character that's three of these types. Hell, you don't even have to use these words to describe your characters. I know words are everything for us bookish types, but also... they're just words. We can all calm the fuck down and keep our asses on the sofa. These are just helpful nuggets to label and identify the ink and paper creatures you're creating. Right, what are the main character development types?

- Dynamic
- Round
- Static
- Symbolic
- Stock

Dynamic

Dynamic characters are those that change dramatically in the story—like the protagonist. Importantly though, these characters don't change until they have to i.e., they're forced to change by the events in the story.

Round

Much like dynamic characters, round characters change during the course of your novel. However, these bad boys are more willing to change without being forced by the plot. They are typically your major side characters who have smaller arcs. Ron and Hermione in *Harry Potter*, Maui from *Moana*, and Haymitch from *The Hunger Games*.

Static

Static means stationary, doesn't change. Which is why these puppies are sometimes called flat characters. They're intentionally flat because they don't need depth.

Static characters don't develop over the course of the book, or if they do, they're very superficial and shallow. Perhaps instead of a personality change they get something physical they wanted. Usually these are minor or cameo side characters. They can be positive supporting characters or vindictive evil ones.

Often, they'll have a small role, won't reveal much about themselves but serve a minor purpose in the plot. Mr. Filch from *Harry Potter* is an example of this type of character, or Timon and Pumba in *The Lion King*.

There's one other type of static character that can appear in fiction. Occasionally, a villain will also be a static character, though I personally find these villains to be flat. Examples of these villains include overlord characters—think Sauron in *Lord of the Rings*.

Symbolic

A symbolic character is representative of your theme or a variation of your theme or something bigger than the face value of your character. They can be dynamic, round, or static. For example, Boo Radley in *To Kill a Mockingbird*.

The Varying Shades of Stock Characters

Contrary to classical explanations, I think there are two shades of stock character. Broadly though, stock characters are those characters that have very distinctive personality traits which are fixed and unchanging.

There are two key types of stock character:

- Functional Stock (archetypes)
- Characterization Stock

Functional stock characters are those that act as what's often known as archetypal characters. For example, Dumbledore from *Harry Potter* and Gandalf from *Lord of the Rings* both act as "mentors." These are functional stock characters—also known as archetypes—because their archetype serves a function in the story but their character as a whole may serve more than just that purpose.

Characterization stock characters, though, are more likely to be minor or sometimes major characters. However, their personality traits are fixed, they're created more for the purpose of dramatizing characterization than for their benefit as an archetype. Examples of these characters include Wednesday Addams from *The Addams Family*, Rex from *Toy Story*, Regina George from *Mean Girls*. The distinction is that whatever the trait is, it makes up a significant portion of their character and also why they're memorable. Wednesday is memorable for never smiling and having a dark and twisted mind. Rex is a giant coward dinosaur and Regina is memorable for being a bitch. It's both their personality and one of their purposes in their stories to act out these characterization aspects, and while their characterization aspects may create conflict or cause problems, it's not part of the story structure in the same fundamental way a mentor would be.

Clarity, Clarity, Clarity

In the film *The Minority Report*, ol' Cruisey is addicted to a drug called Clarity. I always loved that detail. While the drug isn't about getting "mental clarity," I still find the concept of mental clarity as a drug rather appealing. I'm sure you can recall that moment of solidification of your understanding, when the world slows, your eyes bug wide, and everything gets bright and sparkly. I don't know about you, but it's somewhat of a braingasm for me.

Let's clarify *who* we mean when we say "side character" because there's a big old range of them in a story. There are a few ways to break down the concept of "side character" and not all side characters are born equal.

The simplest way of cutting the deck is thus: major, minor, and cameo.

But there are subtle differences between the terms and I want to take a second to explain so you too can experience the braingasming thrill of clarity. If we're going to make this work between us—and I really hope we are—then this is our "meet cute." Here endeth my TED talk on clarity.

1.2 CAMEOS

Cameos are sometimes called "extras" or throwaway characters. They are the briefest stars. I like to think of them as premature ejac... STOP, Sacha.

But...

NO. Sweet Mother of all things bookish, *nooooo*.

Let me start again.

Cameos fly into a story, burn bright for a second, and wink out in a fit of glorious forgetfulness.

According to dictionary.com a cameo is:

"a minor part played by a prominent performer in a single scene of a motion picture or a television play."

Think Stan Lee, the Marvel comic author. Stan, may he Rest In Peace, starred in almost every Marvel movie ever made. He was only in shot for a few brief seconds and then he was gone. In *The Trial of the Incredible Hulk*, he played the role of a jury foreman. In *Thor*, Stan tries to pull the hammer using his truck. In *Captain America: The First Avenger*, he plays an elderly general.

YA (Young Adult) author Alexandra Bracken starred as a doctor in a single scene of her Hollywood book to film adaptation of *The Darkest Minds*. Mary Robinette Kowal slips a cheeky cameo of Doctor Who in her book *The Glamourist Histories*. Mickey and Minnie Mouse appear briefly in *Who Framed Roger Rabbit*.

Cameos are brief, sacrificial little beings. They are born into life to serve a singular function like reporting the status of a character's health or telling the court the jury's decision. Cameos are shoved into the story on a gilded platter ready to be whipped out and slaughtered for the story gods after delivering their one* perfunctory line.

It is what it is. Someone had to take the shitty job, and the cameo got it.

But herein lies the million-dollar question: how much detail do you need for a cameo character?

The answer is, not a lot.

Think about the films you watch. When the hero walks down the street, cameos are the faceless people he walks past. They're in bland unmemorable clothing, with faces fuzzed out in the background. At most, you might recall a couple of things about a cameo. But I doubt it and that's kinda the point.

A great example comes from *The Matrix* movie. There's a famous scene with the woman in the red dress. Neo—the protagonist—is in a simulator, he's walking through the world, the location looks very much like a regular downtown New York street. Busy, and bustling with people. Morpheus (his mentor) is walking slightly ahead of him telling him important information. Everyone in the simulation is in bland black suits, and professional clothes. They're on phones, and carrying brief cases. Everyone looks the same. Morpheus asks whether he's paying attention. He was, until a woman in a red dress walked past him—the only human wearing even a hint of color. Of course he was distracted. Morpheus asks him to look back.

When he does, the woman is gone and an enemy agent is holding a gun to Neo's face. The point in the film is that anyone can be an agent. The point it makes about cameos is that they appear one second and are gone the next. Oh, and the only thing you remember in the *Matrix*—if at all—is that there was some rather attractive lady wearing a bright red dress.

So yes, you can describe their appearance if you want, but cameos aren't around long enough for your reader to remember much about them and frankly, they don't need to. Why fill their brain with useless shit? Stick to giving them the good stuff.

* "One line" is an arbitrary amount. Don't get pedantic with me. I needed a small number and I chose one because... well, it's first. Cameos can, of course, have more than one line. The point is they don't have many.

A Note on Arcs, Subplots, and Labels

Cameos don't need subplots or character arcs. Ever. They don't even need a name. Most of the time the author creates a label for the character. Like the aforementioned woman in the red dress, or perhaps the barman, or the girl with the teddy. Don't get worked up about cameos—sprinkle and run...

1.3 MINOR (OR SECONDARY) CHARACTERS

Moving right on up from cameos are minor characters. Minor characters are sometimes known as secondary characters, but I think "minor" and "major" is a clearer differentiation than "side" and "secondary" or "supporting." So, we're sticking with minor.

Minor characters are but a wee bit more enduring than cameos. Imagine them as a quickie behind the... Wait, no.

Get out of the gutter, Sacha.

Sigh. Fine.

Let's say they're cameo times five. They appear more than once, perhaps a few times maybe a few more than that.

However, while they may look pretty on camera, they are still just an extra in a film. They appear and do their job much like a perfunctory shag—everyone gets what they want, but no one's really satisfied. These babies—note this bit is important —tend to leave no meaningful trace on the story. They could be removed from the book and it have very little impact. Occasionally their role might need to be assigned to another character, especially if they harbor useful information or let a protagonist into a building or some such trivial but needed action. Broadly, most—emphasis on most, because rebel writers break the rules all the goddamn time—of these minor characters could be forgotten just like the cameos.

Minor character roles include bringing information, performing a repetitive role like a barman or receptionist, being a relative that pops up, etc. While their role may be important to the "world" or the magic system or the legal system etc., it has no sway over the story or the protagonist save for a transactional exchange.

Both cameos and minor characters are unlikely to have character arcs. For more on arcs, read Step 6 on arc weaving.

Examples of minor characters include Mr. Filch (the janitor) from the *Harry Potter* series, Wheezy from *Toy Story 2*, Tiny Tim from *A Christmas Carol*, Magda from *The Hunger Games*, Kit Fisto from *Star Wars*, Zed from *Pulp Fiction*.

You're probably scratching your head trying to remember who these characters are. And that's the point. These characters are, for the most part, forgettable. They create a familiar itch in the back of a reader's mind. That sensation of knowing you should remember, but not quite being able to reach the answer. That's why minor characters aren't point of view (POV) characters. POV characters require page time, and depth. Minor characters don't have much of either.

How Much Detail Is Needed for a Minor Character, Then?

More than a cameo, less than a major character.

You should probably describe a minor character and ensure they have a defining characteristic that makes them recognizable enough so they're at least a smidge memorable. After all, your hero and your reader will encounter them more than once and they need enough memorability to create that itch in the reader's mind. Just because they aren't in the story very much, doesn't mean they have to be bland, shapeless, trash bags. Nay, my dear writer, we can do better than that. They can sparkle and shine and glitter like the little desperate-for-attention harlots they are. Which means, unlike cameos, minor characters are more likely to have identified names even if they are as stereotypical as Mike the barman.

Sadly, for these tyrants, no matter how bright they shine, they still aren't going to get much deeper than a golf putt. They don't need to be as fully fleshed out as either your protagonist, antagonist, or your major characters. The chances of needing a backstory are slim to none. You don't need an origin story either unless one or other of those things is highly relevant to the plot. Last, you don't need a wound or flaw from their past and they don't particularly need to have a goal, desire or want either.

Do Minor Characters Need a Character Arc and Subplot?

No.

I'm sure some smart aleck will come up with the one exception of a minor character who has an arc because it resolves a key subplot or does something to support the protagonist. But I'd argue that any character with an arc is dangerously close to "major character" territory and if you're going to get that close then why not do the job properly and make them a major character?

Blows raspberries

Get back in your box smarty pants.

Of course, minor characters can be involved in a subplot, they may even have their own, *very* minor subplot, but broadly speaking... Back. Away. From. The. Subplots. And. Arcs.

It's enough that they exist in your world and flit into and out of a protagonist's story.

Shocking as it may sound, minor characters can be two dimensional, you don't have time to create anything more than the illusion of depth. These guys aren't in the story or affecting the story enough to warrant anything more dimensional.

1.4 MAJOR CHARACTERS

Major side characters are the big leagues of side characters. They are the folks this book is mostly dedicated to. The easiest way to conceptualize the difference is to think of protagonists and major characters as three dimensional and everyone else as two dimensional. As we progress through this book and get deeper into the creation of these chaps, I want you to bear these three—major, minor, and cameo—classifications in mind.

The "Major" Headlines

Major side characters...

- are three-dimensional characters, which means they need depth
- may have a point of view or narrate parts of the story
- usually have subplots dedicated to them
- usually have arcs
- are likely to be rare beasties, in other words, there will only be a handful of them

- represent one angle of the theme

These salacious sideys have a meaningful role to play, shaping and influencing the protagonist. They create conflict and plot problems and help solve them just as frequently. Perhaps they're the catalyst that helps the hero to change or maybe they're one of the obstacles preventing the change. Let's go deeper.

Three-Dimensional Characters

Major side characters are vital to the story in a way that other cameos and minor characters are not. You can lose a pint of blood and survive. Your story can hemorrhage cameos and minor characters and be just fine. But you rip out a kidney, a lung, the intestinal tract, or an aortic valve and you're going to notice something's missing. Major characters form part of the foundations of your story. They're like bones in your story skeleton. They must be three dimensional, so chances are they will have a backstory of their own. Backstory helps to create depth, as does having strengths and flaws, as does having a goal or objective that isn't solely "help the protagonist." How much we see of each of those elements, though, is dependent on two things:

1. How connected the element is to the plot and theme
2. How "major" a side character they are

Majors Represent the Theme

Major characters should also be connected to the theme of your story. While the protagonist represents the answer to the story question—or the theme itself—your major side characters will likely (and probably should) be some variation of the theme too. If your theme is love, it might play out something like this:

- The hero represents "love always wins"
- Major character A represents "love yourself first"
- Major character B represents "I don't need love to be happy"

We'll cover this in depth in Step 2.

Majors May Have POVs or Narrate

Major characters are the ones who are established enough they can have a point of view all for themselves. Perhaps they're a second narrator or maybe they only narrate a few parts of the story. These guys don't *have* to narrate of course, but they should be well developed enough that they *could* narrate. Which means they're well developed enough that should you be so inclined you could create a spin-off series, book, or movie script about them.

Think Ron Weasley and Hermione Granger from the *Harry Potter* series, Trinity from the *Matrix* movie, Grandpa Joe in *Charlie and the Chocolate Factory*, Four from the *Divergent* series, the three ghosts of Christmas in *A Christmas Carol*. All characters we know and love and are sufficiently interesting enough that we'd happily read another story about them.

Majors Have Subplots and Arcs

These major pups need some page time dedicated to them and some sort of arc in order to give you at least the illusion of depth. Imagine trying to watch a dream boy strip through a one-way blind in a torrential downpour—you're going to have to use your imagination a bit... Their arcs and subplots don't need to be complex like the protagonist; in fact, they shouldn't be—otherwise they encroach on protagonist territory. And there can only be one hero after all. But these characters need the semblance of an arc. Take the example from above. Major character A represented "love yourself first." This means they'd start the story focused on loving and putting others first. But by the end of the story, they're empowered and focus on loving themselves before others. Major character B represented "I don't need love to be happy." The most obvious arc here would be starting the story in a relationship and ending it happy and single. Both of which could be resolved in short lines, paragraphs, or longer scenes. The key to note is that their subplots should be connected to the main plot and theme in some way. We will cover this in Steps 3 and 6.

How Many?

Major characters are but one step removed from the protagonist. As a result, unless you're George R.R. Martin or one of those authors who loves a frivolously gargantuan cast, the chances are you'll have a small set of major characters, all who play vital roles in the story.

You need all three types of characters in your novel. It's no good trying to make every bit-part cameo a full-on minor character. You can't have 666 protagonists and you shouldn't have that many supporting characters either—looking at you George.

Major side characters are greedy little munchkins. While they're not the focus of the storyline they are present enough in the story that they're more than a cameo or minor character and this can cause problems for writers when they become divas and attention whores. It means that unless you're writing a book of encyclopedic proportions you don't have time to create a metric fuckton of major side characters.

Significant Marks

There are some other key roles a major character has. First up, major side characters need to **leave a significant mark,** impact or impression on the story. Just like the second in command in a crime book whose tangential waffling helps the protagonist figure out whodunit, your side characters have to add something, change something, impact or influence something so they're adding to the story too. If they're not doing one of those, then they're redundant and that, my pen monkeys, means you can kill your darling. Hack the fucker out. Send them to the slaughter house. Knock the waster on the head and rid yourself of the extra layer of character fat. That, or I suppose if you're feeling less stabby, you could just demote them to minor character status.

Dance with the Hero

Major characters need to interact with the protagonist. If they're a major character then they should be supporting the protagonist. Don't get me wrong, support is used in loose terms here. They could be supporting her by being a ruddy great big obstacle, which ultimately pushes the hero to defeat her flaw. Negative support is still support in this context, because it's pushing her towards her big goal.

If you're being pernickety, you could argue that a character who never appears in the "present time" of a story isn't a major character. But you'd be wrong.

If this major side character is in enough memories or flash backs or mentioned frequently and they have an impact or effect on the protagonist or the plot in the present of the story, then feel free to class them—and consequently treat them—as a major side character.

A great example of this comes from *The Sky Is Everywhere*

by Jandy Nelson. In the book, the protagonist's sister died just before the start of the story. While her sister never appears on the page in the "flesh"—duh, she's dead—the influence she has over the living sister is enormous. Arguably, even though the dead sister is not embodied, she leaves enough of a mark and impact on the story that she's still a side character and a major one too.

Many of the best side characters are memorable. Perhaps this is more of a consequence of the above two points. But your more significant side characters really ought to be memorable because they (a) command so much page time, (b) are well characterized and (c) have a memorable impact on the story, your protagonist, and consequently your reader.

We'll look at how you can do this in later chapters.

Practice Makes Purpose

Major side characters should have a purpose. Two, in fact. One purpose linked to the story and connected to the protagonist—i.e., if they are the protagonist's best friend then they're going to be supporting whatever the protagonist's goal is—and a second purpose or goal reserved just for them and their lives. This helps to give them that additional layer of depth that's important for making them seem real and fleshed out.

Facelifting Major to Minor, Minor to Major

One last question: can you turn a minor character into major character? Why, sure you can, Dorothy. You can flip-flop these puppies up and down, but if you do, make sure you trim or pad the character fat accordingly. You don't want a supposed minor character appearing on all the pages and in all the scenes. That just won't do now, will it?

1.5 HOW MANY MINIONS?

Size Matters...

Not that size winky wink... Another occasion size matters is with the number of characters you're creating. I'm not here to lecture you on the number of characters you should or shouldn't have. A more relevant question is how many characters does your story require?

Harry Potter and the Philosopher's Stone by J.K. Rowling has 131 named characters, *A Game of Thrones* by George R.R. Martin has 218 named characters. *The Eye of the World* by Robert Jordan has 250 named characters. In fact, his *Wheel of Time* series has over 2700 named characters. And then on the other end of the scale you have books like *Hatchet* by Gary Paulsen that for the most part has just one character. Or what of that odd movie by Tom Hanks, *Castaway*, where it's just him and a volleyball head called Wilson for 90% of the movie.

How do you know whether or not you've got the right number of characters? Here are a few questions to help you determine your number:

- Does every character have a clear and distinct function?
- Are any of the characters repeats—i.e., two mentors, two foils etc.—and if yes, can they be merged?
- Are you struggling to find new ways to distinguish characters?
- Do any of the characters blend into each other?
- Do you have scenes where characters are lost in conversations and actions?

If we trek back to our previous structure of cameo, minor, and major characters, I like to think of a collection of characters like Maslow's Hierarchy of Needs[1]. If your characters are a triangle, then on the bottom—the biggest section—are cameos. You'll likely need a swathe of background characters, "crowds," door openers, nameless security guards and so on, to make your story world seem realistic. The mid sections of the triangle are for minor and major characters. Minor characters will sit above cameos in the triangle because there are less of them than cameos but they appear more often. Major characters sit above minor characters in the triangle as the third section. This is because they're heavily involved in the plot, conflict and influencing the protagonist. Which is why there's fewer still of these than minor characters. A handful of them at most. The depth they require means you have to spend time deepening them on the page; you only have a finite number of many pages, which is why you can only have a limited number of major characters.

That leaves the peak of your triangle, which is reserved for your one and only protagonist.

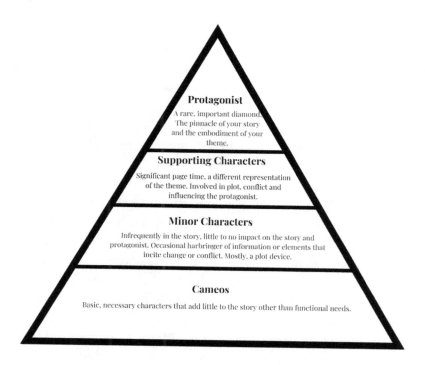

Déjà Duplicate

One error to avoid is duplicate characters. It's one of the most common issues I see with side characters. Perhaps you have two mentors. I can practically hear the "but, but, but one is for the protagonist's royal duties and the other one for their secret magical academia studies." Oh, honey, please. That's still two mentors and unless you have a 20ft-thick solid reason—and they do exist occasionally—then one of those darlin's gotta go. Why? Well, duplicate characters are a waste of real estate. Why have two shallow characters more or less doing the same job when you could go deep and use the real estate to penetrate under the skin of one? And who's to say the royal tutor isn't moonlighting as a magical mentor? It's always more effective to have one character doing a role than two doing the same job under a different guise.

I should point out here that this doesn't mean each character can only have one friend or "ally" in archetype terms. To be clear, the two—or more—allies should be performing different functions in the story. If one is there as the "geek" who can always unearth the information they need at the right time and another ally is there to fill the hero with the confidence they need to undertake the plot challenge, well then, they're performing different roles.

---

1. Maslow's Hierarchy of Needs diagram adapted from A.H. Maslow (1954) *Motivation and Personality*. Harper.

1.6 WHAT DOES A SIDE CHARACTER DO?

We've ironed out what a side character *is*, we know our cameos from our majors. So then, what is a side character's purpose in a plot? What exactly is it that they *do*?

Side characters are little literary sluts. They do many things:

- Work as literary tools / plot devices
- Function as information revealers
- Provide alternative representations of the theme (see Step 2)
- Set the tone for a scene and help to worldbuild
- Create conflict and drive the plot and pace by pushing or pulling the protagonist in different directions (see Step 8)
- Narrate or help the author avoid exposition by presenting in a narrator type form, which helps the writer to show events rather than telling them (see Step 4)

In terms of story structure, side characters provide pillars of support to the protagonist. They are neither who the story is about nor the hero of the story. But they do provide either support or hinderance for your protagonist. They're plot devices and tools to help you create a story that grips your reader. They help to worldbuild, thicken the emotion and tension, and embody the theme.

In the same way an opening chapter's hook is a promise to the reader, so too are your side characters. They're an unspoken, unwritten oath that trouble is coming. Your readers should be able to "read" the mischief your side characters are going to dish out through their shape on the page. Do their actions and words blur and contradict and hint at unspoken darkness, sexy lies, and murderous secrets? Good, they should.

Side Characters as Literary Tools / Plot Devices

Simply, a plot device is any piece of storytelling that's used to move the story forward. By their very nature, side characters are there to further the protagonist's plight. Whether they're bringing information, hindering the protagonist's growth thereby forcing them to adapt and thus grow, or because they're a friend and partner on an epic quest, side characters further the story. If they don't, then behead the wasteful little oiks; they're as useful as a hot turd on a silver platter and nobody needs turds on platters.

How are side characters used as plot devices? Well, the plot device aspect of their functionality is the umbrella that encapsulates everything else they do. The fact they create conflict means they're a plot device, the fact they reveal information... means they're a plot device. The fact they test the protagonist... yep, you guessed it, means they're a plot device. Anything they do that impacts or effects the story is a plot device action.

Side Characters as Narrators

Just because you have a protagonist, doesn't mean they're going to be the narrator. Doctor Watson is the perfect example of this—he narrates the Sherlock Holmes series despite not being the protagonist. Likewise with Jay Kristoff's *Nevernight* in which the narrator is never really revealed; although in an interview[1] Kristoff admits that the narrator is Mercurio—the protagonist's, Mia Corvere's, mentor.

You can get the link to the interview, as well as a bonus side characters checklist, by downloading the free resource booklet at sachablack.co.uk/sidecharacters.

Indeed, it is not uncommon for authors to use multiple POVs in a story, and sometimes they can be alternating tenses such as in the case of *Roseblood* by A.G. Howard, where she uses first person present for the protagonist and third person past tense for the love interest. Though a word of caution here—it can be jarring to the reader unless done incredibly well.

Using multiple character POVs makes it easier to show plot points that one character or another may not have witnessed. But it also makes it harder to keep the story under control. These characters have a tendency to get longer and unwieldy, all of them jostling for their own major plotline.

Another tactic for having either multiple POV characters or a narrator who isn't the protagonist is to keep some distance between the reader and the protagonist. As in the case of Watson and Holmes, you're not privy to any of Sherlock's workings out until they're laid on the page. It creates mystery, intrigue, characterization, and desire for the reader to find out what on earth is going on in the ol' Holmesy head.

Side Characters as Pace Drivers

Let's say you have a lone wolf character. He hates people— hands up, how many of you are nodding at this point? Well stop, dammit. The wolf doesn't have many friends, doesn't even want many friends. See, you're in a sticky situation here; while this is a popular trope—think of many maverick cops or agents in thrillers—there's a glaringly dangerous obstacle for authors.

Not giving your protagonist any characters to interact with makes it incredibly hard to create any kind of pace. Why? Well, for one, dialogue is one of the most effective tools at creating pace. It's a whip-snap back and forth, it changes sentence after sentence, hops between characters, by its very nature it's jerky and rapid fire. The complete opposite of lengthy descriptive prose. And yes, you can have some scenes with single characters and you can use some techniques like enhancing the amount of movement and playing with sentence length and the senses to create some semblance of pace, but it just ain't the same as a good ol' chinwag, folks.

When you have a lone wolf character and you keep him isolated, you're handcuffing yourself. It's almost impossible to create dialogue with a single character without it sounding contrived when the character talks to himself. Be honest, how many of us talk to ourselves out loud? I'm betting not many, sure some of us talk to ourselves but it's usually in our heads—I say usually because there are always exceptions. But unfortunately for you writers, you cannot be the exception; there are very few occasions when a character can talk to themselves and it not sound weird—the odd line, sure, prolonged dialogue, nuh-uh.

You need side characters because they enable your protagonist to have conversations, to engage and banter and talk to others, and this helps the pace of your scenes and story overall.

---

1. https://thegarretpodcast.com/jay-kristoff-nevernight-chronicles/

STEP 1 WTF IS A SIDE CHARACTER? SUMMARY

Where we sprinkled a dash of side and added a dusting of cameo, sniffed clarity like it's a drug, fought combatants, patted our corporately inclined managers on the head, and remembered Stan Lee.

~

- Story is about change. Characters (all of them protagonists and side characters alike) represent and embody this change.
- All characters are the embodiment of the idea behind your story. Some like to call this the theme. Characters draw the idea into reality. They are a metaphor that makes the idea and concept real to us. Characters show us through the detail of their actions, their emotions, and interactions what the idea really means.

Side characters are many things:

- Literary tools / plot devices
- Information revealers
- Alternate representations of the theme
- Tone setters
- Conflict creators
- Drivers of the plot
- Help the author avoid exposition by presenting in a narrator type form which helps the writer to show events rather than telling them

The three types of side character are: major, minor, and cameos:

- **Cameos** are the briefest stars. They play a very short, succinct role, such as a throwaway perfunctory line, opening a door for the protagonist, a throng of faceless beings in a crowd etc.
- **Minor** side characters are a little bit more enduring than cameos. While they appear on a page a few more times than a cameo, they are still just an extra in a film. Minor character roles include bringing information, or performing a repetitive role like a barman or receptionist.
- **Major** side characters are one step removed from the protagonist. They have a meaningful role to play. They shape and sway the protagonist. They create conflict and plot problems and help solve them just as frequently. Perhaps they're the catalyst that helps the hero to change or maybe they're one of the obstacles preventing the change. Major characters should also be connected to the theme of your story. While the protagonist represents the answer to the story question, your major side characters will likely

be some variation of the theme too, but we'll cover this in the next chapter.

- The quantity of each type of side character you have is entirely dependent on the type of story you tell. Broadly speaking, for the average story, it's likely you'll have more cameos than any other type of character. You'll have fewer minor characters but still a good chunk of them. And you'll only have a handful of major characters because of the page time they require to fulfill their role.

Questions to Think About

1. What are your favorite side characters from your genre?
2. Identify three major, minor, and cameo side characters from the genre you write.

STEP 2 THE WEB OF CONNECTIVITY AND THEME

2.0 THE WEB OF CONNECTIVITY AND THEME

Where we discuss my deepest spidery fear, we realize it's all a big ball of connection, dance with hourglass figures, experience nipple cripples, and build penis turrets.

Spoiler warnings for books: *I, Robot* by Isaac Asimov, *To Kill a Mockingbird* by Harper Lee, *The Hunger Games* by Suzanne Collins, *Harry Potter and the Philosopher's Stone* by J.K. Rowling, *The Hunger Games* by Suzanne Collins, and *The Scent of Death* by Sacha Black

Spoiler warnings for movies: *Romeo and Juliet, Bridget Jones's Diary*

If you take but one thing from this book, let it be this chapter. This is where I want you to focus your understanding of side characters. Pull off your spectacles, roll up thine sleeves, we're about to mud wrestle in character soup; prepare for black eyes, vagina kicks, ball squeezing, and nipple cripples.

A Brief Explanatory Interlude of the Web of Connectivity

I don't like to pick favorite children—*that's a lie, what's a deviant overlord supposed to do if not pick an heir?*—but in *10 Steps to Hero,* my favorite chapter is the web of connectivity. This is the concept that each element of a book is threaded together like the strands of a spider's web.

> "In a finished book, each part—the characters, theme, twists, arcs, and subplots—are all seamlessly woven together. A published novel has the sexy look of an hourglass figure in a skin-tight dress with no visible panty line." Sacha Black, *10 Steps to Hero: How to Craft a Kickass Protagonist.*

In a spider's web, every strand, whilst woven separately and standing alone in and of itself, is also intricately connected to every other thread in the web. It's how a spider knows while sitting in the top right-hand corner, that something just flew into the bottom left. The whisper thin vibrations ripple through all of the threads. Much as the hairy critters give me the jitters, I must confess, every web is a feat of spidery "Gestaltism" genius.

But what in literary-hell's name is Gestaltism?

It's a psychological concept that states the whole is more than the sum of its parts—much like a book, wouldn't you say?

Gestaltism is my own personal obsession. I am deeply fasci-
nated by the concept that something designed to be one thing
can also create another just because of its constituent parts.
That is some next level mind jiggery fuckery.

When you get close to a book, all you see are the words and
sentences, the big characters, and the chapter titles. But step
back, take in the story in all its glory, and all-of-a-spangly-
sudden, it's so. Much. More. It's a tangled web of interconnect-
edness. It's theme and epiphanies, it's messages and subtext, it's
a thriving, pulsing bag of magical juice, and glittering urges.

And the side characters? Well, they're one of the silky
threads connecting them all.

Scratch your noggin' a sec, in section 1.0, I said *"Side characters are pillars of theme. They are the arteries in a protagonist-heart.
They are perspectives and viewpoints."* This is where that becomes
relevant.

Let's say in a spider's web, the protagonist is the crusty
conglomeration of tangled threads at the center. That means
each major thread around the outside—the pillar threads
attached to branches and fence posts and leaves—which are
vital for stability and structural integrity are... bet you can't
guess... go on, I dare ya...

Oh yes, my brethren, those web pillars are the side
characters.

Without them, the web collapses, just like your story.

Oof, I need a lie down, I'm all moist and clammy with
excitement and perspiration.

What Do Pillar Threads Mean for Story?

As we know, each thread is connected in a web, but there
are some threads with more connections than the rest—the
pillar threads. These threads have connections left and right all
the way down to the core of the web where the protagonist sits.

Which means, your side characters should be connected to the protagonist and multiple elements in your story. Woven like your Nanna's best jumper.

Let's take a look at how and why those puppies connect in the rest of Step 2.

2.1 WHAT IS THEME?

The Sacred Connection of Character Beasties to Theme Beasties

Why am I talking about the side characters in relation to theme? Simply, all characters are metaphors for the theme, each of them in their own delightfully unique way.

Now granted, some people discover their theme as they write, that's cool, you can refine it in your edits. But if you want a solid side character, at some point you need to connect them to the theme. Your side characters should be a representation of your greater whole. By that I mean a representation of the web of connectivity.

Sticks trident in the ground

Fires flare gun

Now, listen up, everyone knows the protagonist is the embodiment of the theme. But the trick most avid writers miss is that your side characters should represent the theme too. Just a different aspect of the theme than your protagonist.

This is one of those icky, tricky, sticky points because, of course, you can get away with a character who *isn't* intimately connected to your theme. But then lots of stories don't do this and don't do that, and there are some stories that are literary masterpieces and some that are pure unadulterated pulp fiction fun. It's all fine, there are readers for every kind of story, it's a big fucking world out there, people. There's a fetish for everyone.

In my humblest of opinions as a lowly story craft nut, a book tends to feel... just that little bit *more* when the side characters are all up close and intimate with the theme. I'm not saying they need to wham-bam-thank-you-ma'am the theme, but you know... a casual bit of hand holding would be good.

If you want to write next level books, this is one way to up your game. When your characters are all part of a greater whole, they give your reader that sense of connection—the feeling of greater meaning and the experience of seamlessly woven threads throughout the book. You're far more likely to induce a book hangover once they've turned that final page doing this, than you are if your characters aren't connected to anything other than their personal orifices.

What Is Theme?

I used to despise theme. But I'm a rebel, even against myself, and now I adore theme. Personally, I like starting a book knowing what the theme of the story is. I wrote my first series not knowing it and honestly, it made it much harder. I can hear the muted cries of panic. Writers everywhere are snapping pencils, sacrificing printer paper. But no, calm down baby Yoda, *you* don't have to start with theme. As long as you're doing all the work, whipping your prose, twerking... sorry, tweaking your characterization, who gives a tiny weeny violin-sized shit when you're figuring out the theme. Create it before you write, edit it in during your second draft, craft it while sat on the loo straining for your life for all I care. The most important thing is getting to the end of the book. How you do that is no one's business other than yours.

I don't particularly enjoy the editing process; my favorite bit of writing is the vomit-draft stage. In order to stave off reams of edits, I like to start with a fair amount of information especially about my characters so I'm not having to make gargantuan changes to plot or characters in the editing phase. But you know how these insolent characters work, sometimes they barrel in and fuck shit up for us. Thus, in summary, you do you, honey.

Shall we address the giant mythological unicorn that is theme?

When "theme" is wafted into a hall full of writers, the usual response is a tightening of sphincters, a mildly glazed look washing over faces and a strangely sour odor emanating from armpits.

Theme is all big and scary and hard, right.

But is it though?

Come now rebels, let me slide my ink-stained arm around you and tell you it's all going to be okay.

"It really is."

Theme isn't big and scary, it's just another device, another tool to convey the story you really want to tell. Theme is not a holy grail or a mythical unicorn. It's not difficult, it's not a trickster. It is what your story is about.

I don't mean boy meets girl and they fall in love—that's plot. I mean what your book is *really* about.

If a book were a body, the plot would be the skin, the bit you see, the aesthetics. The theme of your story is the underlying meaning, or in "body terms," the heart of your book. Theme is the philosophical, moral, or psychological idea the author wants to convey through their story. That makes it sound like the retirement spiel of an overly pompous, intensely stuffy professor, but it doesn't have to be. The point, I suppose, is that theme is what's beneath the surface.

Perhaps the most common confusion with theme is the "moral lesson." The idea and the lesson are a luscious Venn diagram of connection.

A theme could be a viewpoint, a deeper commentary or statement on a topic. For example, Isaac Asimov's *I, Robot,* theme is about humanity and its need for superiority and control; arguably though, the lesson the characters learn is that humans aren't clever enough to anticipate all the consequences of their inventions.

One way to look at this is that the theme is an exploration of the question, and the moral lesson is the answer the characters find and learn.

Ultimately, theme tends to be some exploration of the universal human condition. Like:

- Good versus evil—think *Harry Potter* or *To Kill a Mockingbird*
- Love—any romance novel ever, like *Bridget Jones* or romance and tragedy like *Romeo and Juliet*
- Sacrifice—*The Hunger Games*

Those are just the most obvious themes. Themes can range from the cost of human connection to courage, revenge, inequality and everything in-between. Perhaps I'm oversimplifying. While you absolutely can have a one-word theme, because theme embodies itself in a lesson, it tends to become a sentence or so. For *Romeo and Juliet,* it could be one of many sentences: love is violence. How far would you go for love? The line between love and obsession etc.

Hopefully, you're starting to get a picture of theme. Can you have a book without a theme then? Probably? Possibly? I don't recommend it though.

Why?

Because theme is the golden thread that's woven through every chapter, every scene, protagonist, and side character. It's the gestalt web that connects all things novel. We know your hero is an expression of the theme. Your villain, then, is an expression of the anti-theme. Which means your side characters are expressions of theme possibilities. No matter whether you spill it intentionally from your fingertips or you accidentally choke it up on the page. It will be there. If you were a fisherman making a net by flinging bits of string around the dock, eventually you'd have something resembling a coughed-up hairball of a net. Chances are it would have missed loops, be knotty as fuck, and probably unfit for purpose. But it would exist!

With all story elements, it's better to intentionally weave those threads and connections; it makes them much stronger because the knots have a purpose.

How Do You Come up with Theme?

Lots of writers struggle when trying to come up with their theme. One easy way to combat this is to start with whatever is most universal in your story.

- Look at your characters, plot, subplots, and climax. What is the protagonist having to decide or choose in the big climax scene? What aspects of that choice are universal to all humans irrespective of race, gender, sexuality, age, or any other demographic?
- Putting your entire book to the side for a moment, is there something you'd like your readers to go away with after? What would you like them to ponder long after your story fades in their mind?
- This is usually seen as a sin—though frankly, if

we're going to commit sins, I can think of far better ones to commit—but if you're really struggling, you could give your earlier drafts to a friend—a writer—and ask them if they can pick out the theme for you.

- Go back to your story hook. How did your story start? What was the premise? Examine the premise and extrapolate out your theme.

Right, let's look deeper at how characters and theme smush together in the frothy boiling pot of character sludge.

2.2 CONSTRUCTING A THEMATIC CAST

I purposefully used the word construction because creating a novel is somewhat of a construction task. Especially when you're creating a cast of characters to go with the plot.

Let's pretend we're all rich enough to build the house of our dreams. Would you let the architect and builders go off half-cocked building and designing whatever they liked in your house? I doubt it—what if they thought penis-shaped turrets were appropriate?

CHRIST KAREN, THINK OF THE NEIGHBOURS.

fans self

No, if you were building the house of your dreams, you'd make sure your brickwork matched the stone slabs they used for the path and the driveway. You'd make sure there were windows in every room and that the carpet wasn't some gaudy shade of puke. I'd bet you'd check every inch of that house before you handed over your hard-earned cash.

Well with novels, you're the builder and readers are handing over their cash. We ought to make sure your construction skills are on point, shouldn't we? No penis-shaped chapters, unless you're writing erotica, in which case, as you were.

Character, Plot, and Theme

Character and plot are not separate. Character is plot. And side characters are... well, characters. Which means they're plot too. Side characters are mechanisms for exploring the plot, obstacles, and themes from a different angle than your protagonist.

As I've mentioned, one of the best ways to differentiate your side characters from each other is to make them a differing representation of the theme. But how the hell do you do that?

Well, your side characters can connect to the theme in one of a few ways:

- By being a positive representation of the theme
- A negative representation of the theme
- A flip flop arc from a negative to positive representation of the theme
- A flip flop arc from positive to negative representation of the theme

What does that look like in practice?

Theme: love is enough.

Positive representation: Jennifer is sick of looking after her family. She's miserable in her life. But Jennifer is in a traumatic car accident; she, her husband, and daughter survive, but Jennifer's cousin dies. This makes Jennifer realize she wants nothing more than to look after her family and spend quality time with them.

Negative representation: Clare loves Charles, but Charles is never satisfied no matter how much he manipulates Clare into

the lover he wants. In the end, Clare leaves and Charles is
alone.

Positive to negative: Julie's husband has an affair. After trying
hard to make things work, she decides love isn't enough and
she wants more from her life. She ends the marriage and skips
off into the sunset as a happy, fulfilled, single woman off on
travel adventures.

*Note here that while the outcome for Julie is positive empower-
ment, it's still a negative representation of the theme. The theme
implies that Julie should have been happy at the end because love is
always enough.*

Negative to positive: James, suave bachelor and permanent
singleton, never wants to settle. But after a bout of illness that
keeps him house-bound for six weeks with no visitors, he realizes how alone he is. Then he meets Lauren, a fun, loving and
devoted family girl. He commits to Lauren, realizing that love is
enough to make him happy and not feel trapped.

Arcs Dance with Theme

When looking at the theme, your first decision is whether
your characters are a positive or negative embodiment of it. If
they're a negative embodiment, will they prevent the hero from
achieving his goal? Or will they be a catalyst for showing the
protagonist what he doesn't want to become?

If the side character is a positive embodiment of the theme,
then the same question applies. Will the positivity show the
hero what he wants to become and therefore help push him
towards his goal? Or will it teach him a lesson? Will it show him
that he wants something else even though everyone in his life
thinks it's for the best?

In any story you often have one or more side characters representing the following different relationships with the theme:

- A character who always sticks to the theme truth or theme message
- A character who always sticks to a theme lie; i.e., in the above example, love is not enough
- A character who moves from believing a truth about the theme to believing a lie
- A character who moves from believing a lie about the theme to believing a truth

Of course, you may have other variations on those, but they are a framework when constructing your characters.

Here's a worked example from the book I'm currently writing, *The Scent of Death* (note all references to the book are written in British English):

Mallory Mortimer is the protagonist and is hell-bent on saving everyone he loves. The one-word theme is "saving," the theme sentence is something along the lines of: *if you love someone, you should save them.* This is what Mallory embodies. But let's look at how I've represented variations of that theme with the other characters.

- Frank [surname pending] is gay and in the closet and struggling to come out in order to save himself. *Theme representation—A character who moves from believing a lie about the theme to believing a truth.*
- Pearl Rafferty [the love interest] is strong and independent and doesn't want saving because she can do it herself thank you very much. *Theme representation—A character who always sticks to a theme lie, i.e., Pearl doesn't need saving.*

- Pearl's mum wants to save kids by fostering them. *Theme representation—A character who always sticks to the theme truth or theme message—Pearl's mum will stop at nothing to save the kids.*
- Pearl's father works for an environmental charity and is trying to save the earth. *Theme representation —much like his wife, Pearl's father is saving the planet instead of kids and thus is a character who always sticks to the theme truth or theme message.*
- Mal's mother is an alcoholic and can't save herself unless she chooses to. *Theme representation—like Mal, his mother is a character who moves from believing a lie about the theme to believing a truth. Mal's mother didn't believe she was worthy of saving no matter who she loved or who loved her.*
- Mal's father wants to save his soul by asking for forgiveness. *Theme representation—this is a tricky one because Mal's father is a poking rod I'm using to make Mal question his morals. On the outside, Mal's father is a very negative character, but in the story, he's actually a character who always sticks to the theme truth or theme message, as no matter his past or his past relationships, he's trying to save both Mal and himself.*

Mal himself, like a lot of protagonists, represents a character who moves from believing a lie about the theme to believing a truth.

Every single character mentioned above is a twist on the theme. All of them are trying to save something, whether that's saving themselves, the environment, children, or actively trying to not be saved. Each character has been purposefully crafted and chosen to shed light on a different side of the theme. Each of their resolutions has a different outcome on the theme. But all of them, without doubt, are connected to the theme itself and therefore the protagonist too. Now there are many other characters such as police officers, vets, Mal's teachers, etc., who are all minor characters and therefore there to fulfill plot roles rather than have a deeper symbolism or connection to the theme.

Though, when you think about it, police are there to help and save people, vets save animals, and teachers, well... I won't give you that spoiler.

In Which You Give Characters Meaning

Another of those big questions I get asked is:

"How do I make side characters relevant? How do I give characters meaning and make them fulfill a role?"

Let's take the characters I mentioned from *The Scent of Death*. The first thing you can do is decide how they connect to the theme. Be that positive, negative, or neutrally.

If they're connected to the theme, and a major side character, then they're going to have to answer their own thematic question. The very essence of answering their thematic question is a role and gives the characters purpose and meaning. In terms of *The Scent of Death* example, let's look at how they have meaning and how they're answering the theme question:

- Frank is gay, in the closet, and struggling to come out in order to save himself. His theme representation is moving from believing a lie about the theme to believing a truth. His theme question that gives him meaning is: *can he come out and save his mental health and identity no matter the consequences?*
- Pearl Rafferty doesn't want saving because she can

do it herself. Her theme representation is sticking to a theme lie. Which means her question is: *will Pearl let Mal save her or will she save herself?*

- Pearl's mum wants to save kids by fostering them. Her theme rep was sticking to the theme truth which is why her question is: *can she defeat the legal system in order to save the kids?*
- Pearl's father cares about the environment. He reps the theme the same way Pearl's mom does—always sticking to the theme truth. The question that helps give his character meaning is: *can Pearl's father save the environment?*
- Mal's mother is an alcoholic; she represents moving from believing a lie to a truth. Her question, then, is: *can she forgive herself and get treatment?*
- Mal's father's theme representation is sticking to the theme truth. His question is: *does he love Mal enough to save his relationship or will he return to his old ways?*
- Which leaves the protagonist. Mal's question could be framed in a couple of ways: *if I love someone, should I save them? Or can I save everyone I love?*

Each of these questions elicits a subplot, a purpose for them to be there and a question for them to answer which will give meaning to their character.

Your job, as author, is to weave them all together so they're part of the same plot. You do this by making sure the subplots intersect each other. For example, with Frank's need to come out, Pearl could push him to tell his parents. Or perhaps Pearl's mother has a chat with Frank one evening when the gang are together watching movies. Maybe Frank is having an argument with Mal when his parents overhear Mal saying, "Just tell them you're gay." Any of these would work and all of them connect multiple side characters together.

To weave side character plots together in the most effective way possible, consider how you can create conflict between the characters and in relation to each of their goals and theme questions.

- Do they have differing opinions?
- Do their goals conflict directly?
- Does the timing of two characters' goals conflict?

In the last example, if Frank was having an argument with Pearl, and his parents found out he was gay, that would cause lots of conflict between him and Pearl and consequently for Mal as the middle man between his girlfriend and best friend.

You'll notice too that of all the questions listed above, the biggest is Mal's. Can he save *everyone* he loves? Every side character's question is very specific to them, it's narrower, more niche, and a more focused issue. Mal's is the theme question itself: *can you save everyone you love?*

Of course, that's not to say you can't have a super niche question for your protagonist. It's just that no matter what the protagonist's problem or question is, it needs to supersede every other character's by being the main theme question. The protagonist's story *is* the story.

Another crucial point to add is that the majority of side character questions should be answered before the protagonist's. Why? Because as each of these character's resolutions come to fruition, Mal, as the protagonist, will witness their outcome, and that in turn, will influence his thoughts on answering his own question. Now, of course, you may well have a character or two who answers their question in the epilogue or after the resolution. That's fine. But it will help the story flow to have the majority of your side character stories answered before the climax.

You can get the side characters checklist to help you craft

theme into your characters by visiting: sachablack.
co.uk/sidecharacters

STEP 2 THE WEB OF CONNECTIVITY AND THEME SUMMARY

- Where we discussed my deepest spidery fear, realized it's all a big ball of connection, danced with hourglass figures, experienced nipple cripples, and built penis turrets.
- Theme tends to be an exploration of the universal human condition.
- The web of connectivity is the concept that each element of a book is threaded together like the threads of a spider's web. Each part of a novel—the characters, theme, twists, arcs, and subplots—are all seamlessly woven together. The pillar threads responsible for stability and structural integrity in a web represent your side characters.
- All characters are metaphors for the theme, each of them in their own delightfully unique way.
- Theme is what your story is about. A simple way to look at this is that the theme is an exploration of the question, and the moral lesson is the answer the characters find and learn. Ultimately, theme tends to

be some exploration of the universal human condition like love, good versus evil, or sacrifice.
- To come up with theme, study your characters, plot, and subplots. What aspects of them are universal to all humans? Examine the choice your hero is making in the climax. Decide the message you'd like your readers to go away with. Or start with your hook and see if you can work out what question connects to it.

Characters can represent the book theme in a variety of ways:

- A positive representation of the theme
- A negative representation of the theme
- A flip flop arc from a negative to positive representation of the theme
- A flip flop arc from positive to negative representation of the theme

In any book, you usually have a character representing the theme in all of the following ways:

- A character who always sticks to the theme truth or theme message
- A character who always sticks to a theme lie, i.e., in the above example, love is not enough
- A character who moves from believing a truth about the theme to believing a lie
- A character who moves from believing a lie about the theme to believing a truth

- To give your characters meaning, ensure their subplots are forcing them to answer a thematic question that's a variation of the protagonist's. And remember, your protagonist should always have the biggest question.

Questions to Think About

1. Examine one of your favorite books from your genre, can you identify the theme?
2. Now identify how each of the major side characters represents that theme.

STEP 3 FLESH AND BLOOD

3.0 FLESH AND BLOOD

Where we Frankenstein our characters, have testicles for ears and nipples for eyes, spit story seeds, play with equations, experience flashbacks, and foist foibles on ourselves.

Spoiler warning for books: *The Invisible Life of Addie LaRue* by V.E. Schwab, *Harry Potter* series by J.K. Rowling, *The Hunger Games* by Suzanne Collins, *Fifth Season* by N.K. Jemisin, *Meat Market* by Juno Dawson, *Northern Lights* by Philip Pullman, *Six of Crows* by Leigh Bardugo, *A Darker Shade of Magic* by V.E. Schwab

Spoiler warning for movies: *The Matrix, Up, Inside Out, Toy Story, Cars, Ocean's Eleven*

Spoiler warning for TV shows: *Dexter, Thirteen Reasons Why* (book also referenced by Jay Asher), *America's Got Talent* 2015

Left unchecked, your side characters can create carnage with your story. Why? Because the devious little fuckers like to steal the limelight. It's a problem. Their personalities start as fledgling seeds, spat from the core of your story brain. And then they become weeds. They grow and root and bury themselves so intimately into your story you can't get them out; suddenly none of your readers give two shitsicles about your hero because your side character is much more fun.

Your side characters aren't locked down by your book's plot. They don't need to overcome obstacles, they're free to just *be*. They get to be themselves but on acid and psychedelic unicorn poops. They're practically unhinged and it's exciting and glorious and no one is going to blame you if you get carried away with your little side muffins.

But, although it pains me to say it, keep them in check we must, and thus, as we start to build our little beasties, we're going to talk through some principles.

I like to think of side characters as the support walls in a house. If you take one of those out you better be sure you replace it or the whole house is unstable. Here are some principles for building those supporting walls.

In this section, I'll give you a brief overview of some important tricks to bear in mind, then we'll dive into detail of how to implement them.

Wet Rags and Limp Bizkit

If you're too young to remember the band Limp Bizkit, then thank you for making me feel old, I shall take my haggard ass back to bed and weep.

A cardinal sin in side character creation is creating side characters that have no impact—in other words, wet rags. It doesn't matter whether they have a positive or negative effect on the story and protagonist, but they do need to have an effect. Otherwise, what the fuck are they doing in your plot, sunshine? Probably a whole lot of fucknothing.

Alongside these glorious beasties needing to have a

purpose, they need to *do* something to meddle with the plot too. Otherwise, they're useless and should be slaughtered and proffered to the literary gods along with your other offerings.

In life as well as in fiction, it's a truism that we understand and learn the most about people by watching and observing what they do, right? If you catch someone slipping a box of pregnancy tests inside their pocket and sneaking out the shop door, it tells you something about that person.

This is key for fiction. If your side characters hop on to the page, and hang around occasionally scratching their ass, picking their nose, and rubbing their heads but not helping to advance the plot, then something is wrong. These guys need to be active.

It's through your side characters' consistent actions that you as the author reveal their nature to the reader.

That said, there's something else you need to bear in mind. While yes, details need to be imparted to the reader to describe action, there's a line. Too much narration and description of actions will slow the pace of your story, some types of description more than others. For example, when you need to world-build, the natural tendency is to insert a paragraph or three of detailed, beautiful, chunky description. But this is the type of description that can slow the pace of your story.

A better way to include the description, keep the pace of your prose and deepen characterization is to allow your character to interact with the elements of the world you're describing. This keeps the description active through interaction. Usually, writers think this means only the protagonist can interact with the world, but oh no, fair maidens. Your side characters can interact with it too.

One of my dear writing friends wears a tattoo on her arm. It says this:

$$E + R = O \text{ (Event + Reaction) = Outcome}$$

What, pray tell, does that mean?

I'm glad you asked.

Jack Canfield writes about this concept. He argues that every outcome you experience is actually the summed conclusion of whatever the event was and your reaction to it. In other words, event plus reaction equals outcome. It makes complete sense in fiction as well as reality. We curate our character's reactions so that they spin off and spiral down before they can come up for air and find the right path. But the point is, these characters are reacting to whatever event has happened in the plot.

It's the case for side characters that their personality is the summation of their actions. We are what we do. Which is why it's important to think about the behaviors and emotions your side characters display. Using action to show traits is the fastest way to create a robust side character personality.

Ask your characters why the details they're describing are important to them. Does it jog a memory? Does it make them feel an emotion? Do they have a visceral reaction? Why people?

Tell me why.

Tell the reader.

Tell your Nanna's lap dancing toy boy.

JUST TELL SOMEONE, dammit.

We want to know because chances are you're going to reveal an aspect of their personality or their background. But you're also allowing them to continue moving and interacting with the world and therefore you're keeping movement, aka action going, and thus your story still has pace. Why does this work? Because you're allowing your character and therefore your reader to physically experience the piece of your world. God, I need a lie down it's so sexy.

Details, Schmetails

Too much detail in a character's description when they're nothing more than a bit-part is overkill. There's an order to these things. The bigger the character the more detail-glitter you can sprinkle on your story. But for the cameos and once-seen fellows, then a brief description, if at all, is fine.

There's another reason it's overkill—your reader doesn't need to know the exact number of toe hairs your protagonist's BFF has. Your side characters have limited page time. Logically then, focusing on a small collection of salient, interesting, and quirky details will convey far more about their personality than trying to capture every inch of their skin, clothing, inside leg measurement, and number of pubic hairs.

More to the point, readers will get overwhelmed with lengthy descriptions, and some will forget them anyway. When there's too many characters that the details get blurred and mashed up, it's frustrating for the reader because they can't remember Fred from Jim, and that makes the story hard to follow.

But equally, you need to choose one detail, something unique about each side character that you can play on. That becomes your side character's "je ne sais quoi." It's what makes them stand out and what makes them memorable. Like Iron Man's suit, or Sherlock Holmes's pipe. It's the thing you can hang your character on. Whatever you choose needs to be unique to that character alone. It needs to set them apart from the rest of the cast.

Double Time, Bitches

One of the pillars of good story telling is making everything work twice for you. You want your description to show you what a character looks like but you also want it to tell you something about that character's personality too.

Sherlock Holmes has a pipe, that tells you he smokes, but

it's a symbolic nod to the fact he's an addict as well. Here is another example:

"...Adeline has decided she would rather be a tree, like Estele. If she must grow roots, she would rather be left to flourish wild instead of pruned, would rather stand alone, allowed to grow beneath the open sky. Better that than firewood, cut down just to burn in someone else's hearth." *The Invisible Life of Addie LaRue* by V.E. Schwab.

This quote is from very early in the book and while on the surface level it could be taken as a simple description, it's much more. Addie spends the vast majority of the book alone, she's unable to grow roots, and when she does find someone she can do that with, she's cut down before they take hold, Luc cuts her down and burns her. This is a description but it's filled with meaning and metaphor and foreshadowing for the rest of the story still to come.

When you make your descriptions work for you in this way, you create a sense of full circle completeness at the end of your story that oftentimes gives readers a book hangover.

Relevancy Is King

One of the principles of characterization is that you should never show the reader anything that isn't relevant. Why? Because what you as the author find interesting is little more than hyperbole to the reader. The reader hasn't come for you, the author, they've come for your characters. They want to know what's pertinent and relevant to your character. When you add trivial details that don't work double time, and don't reveal something more about your characters or the story or the setting etc., you're wasting precious words, page time, and opportunities to make your story work doubly hard for you.

This goes for characters too. Every side character must be relevant. They must play their part and give something to the plot. If they don't, hack 'em out, amputate the papule, and move on.

These are the principles I want you to bear in mind as we make our way through the rest of this book. Your side characters need to:

- Engage with the world
- Impact the story
- You need to make your descriptions work double for you
- Show their personalities through their actions
- Make sure you have identified each side character's "je ne sais quoi"

3.1 A SIDE CHARACTER'S WHY

The Chosen One Fan Girl

Every protagonist will need an inner circle or group of friends. But there's an easy trap to fall into. If you purpose-build your inner circle, you still need to make sure each of those characters has a reason for being in the book, and that purpose can't be wiping the protagonist's ass or carrying their handbags. This isn't fan girl central here people, we're not in protagonist comic con. This is serious business; we're writing books and shit. Characters that exist solely for the protagonist are super cringe.

Of course, part of that reason for existing in the book should be connected to the protagonist, but these side characters need their own goals and lives outside the protagonist's story.

Why?

That's how you make them rounded and believable.

If your side characters don't have these elements, they can read flat, dull and like they're plot puppets created for the sole purpose of furthering the protagonist's agenda or the plot itself.

Sounds a little skin crawly, right? Good, because it is. It's lame, limp, and frankly made of cat-wee cardboard.

Scene Why

Not only should each of your side characters have a reason for being in the book itself, they should have a reason for being in each and every scene they appear in. Got someone flapping on the periphery of a scene? Hack the arm off. Cut them out of that scene. They need to serve a purpose. They need to *do* something in every scene. You can notice these flappy character threads because there will be a giant conversation happening and when you read back through the scene, a character will pop back up out of nowhere.

It'll go something like this:

Enter a group of people. Ol' Freddie boy—our new side character—waltzed in with the group of characters at the start of the scene. There's a deep and meaningful conflab between Vanessa, Sarah, and James about who touched Vanessa's tits when the power went out. Freddie is nowhere to be seen and certainly not joining in the conversation. Freddie seems to have fucked off somewhere. But wait... It's the end of the scene and Vanessa confesses that no one actually touched her tits, it was just wishful thinking. Freddie has magically reappeared and the group exit the room.

If a side character is in a scene—you'd better make damn sure there's a solid reason why they're there and they've showed up suited and booted ready to give their best performance, and not as a passive listener to Vanessa's titty confession.

When you're reviewing your manuscript, make sure every character is doing something, saying something, bringing something, discovering something, or engaging in some way with the action, emotion, and conflict that's happening in the scene.

Life Why

Your side character needs a life outside the protagonist's core plot. This creates the illusion of a full life and therefore a more rounded character.

If you or I were a character, our stories wouldn't have just one plot thread. Sure, many of you reading would have a main plot about writing. I suspect that's why we were all put here, to leave our mark on the world in the form of scrawled words, late nights, and pudgy ink-stained fingers. But that wouldn't be our only plot line, we'd have hundreds of the things. The travel thread and summer romance that got closed off because when we came back home, we started martial arts and fell for our instructor. Or what about the secret physics fetish we harbor late at night reading all about quantum entanglement. We aren't just our soul's purpose. We're more than the words we pour on to the page. And your side characters should be too.

They need things in their lives that aren't circling the main plot. What else is going on in their life? It's these details that bring them to life, make them seem like they have a life outside the protagonist.

Why is that important? Because otherwise, they look like a carbon cut out designed solely to further or hinder the protagonist's goal. And while that *is* their purpose in story structure terms, it's both trite, boring, and wholly unrealistic for the plot and characterization if they only serve the hero.

In the *Iron Man* films, Pepper Pots becomes the CEO of Stark Industries, taking over from Tony so that he can fulfill his role as an Avenger. But this means she develops her own life, schedule, and independence. Meaning she doesn't always agree with Tony—especially when his decisions affect the company that she now runs. This gives her depth and creates conflict when she then says no to him or disagrees with what he's saying.

Your side characters should have a life outside the protagonist, like Pepper does.

Make references to these lives, let them cause problems for the protagonist and the plot. Figure out your side character's wants and desires. Is your character working a job? Are they too busy to help the protagonist with a mission because they have their own work, problem, or an audition? This gives them flesh.

Note that while it's important to reference these elements of their lives, you don't need to let it take over the plot. It's enough to reference, insinuate, and suggest.

Pepper is not the protagonist and, therefore, while she's always in "work attire" and holding a clipboard—references and suggestions—she doesn't take over all of her scenes talking about the ins and outs of CEO'dom. No, her job happens off screen for the most part. When she comes on screen, she's there to talk to Tony about the important bits and then his story role takes over again. References and suggestions are enough to give the illusion of another life. The reader will fill in the gaps and infer the rest.

Other examples of side characters with external-to-the-plot lives include Hermione from *Harry Potter* who spends her time focusing on getting the best grades she can get. Morpheus from *The Matrix* wants to find "The One." In the movie *Up*, Russell wants to get his scouts badge for helping older people, and in *The Hunger Games*, Peeta just wants to survive.

Protagonist Why

Okay, okay, I've labored the point that your side characters need a why outside of your protagonist. But equally, they do need to be connected to and supporting the protagonist's "why" too.

It's important to recognize that while we do get hints of

Pepper's own life and the role she plays as CEO off screen, her job is still intimately connected to the protagonist and his journey. She literally takes over a role he used to do in order to enable him to go off and undertake his adventures as protagonist.

While not every author is going to give their side character's a spin-off series, the structure of the Avengers movies serves as a fantastic analogy for general character structure.

Each Avenger character has their own film which explains their own why, their own purposes and back stories. Think of these as side character spin-offs. And yet, in the final couple of films, all the side characters unite together in a singular plot about the antagonist. Their "why's" converge and their goal is to rid the world of Thanos. This bigger plot is no longer about T'Challa's cousin, or Tony's dad and Stark industries, it's not about Thor's ego or family history and it's not about super soldiers or Captain America's lost lover. All of those aspects remain relevant as they shape the movies, the decision making and actions, but it's not *what* the story is about.

Let's look at each of the side characters I mentioned in the last section because while each of their why's are separate to the protagonist's goal, they are also intricately linked:

- Harry wants to defeat Lord Voldemort—his purpose. But Hermione's desire to know everything leads her to constantly find key bits of information that let Harry and the team defeat the bad guys.
- Morpheus is determined to find "The One" (his purpose) and in doing so, he finds Neo who is the protagonist (and The One).
- Russell wants to complete his volunteering work and help an elderly person and in doing so, he helps Carl Frederickson—the protagonist—to achieve his goal of reaching paradise falls.

- Peeta just wants to survive the games, and in helping Katniss to survive he forms an unbreakable bond that ultimately saves the pair of them.

You can see that while each of these side characters has their own purpose and wants, they're still linked to the protagonist.

3.2 PERFECTLY FLAWED

Perfect Characters

Here we meet Perfect Pete. No one likes him because he's an arrogant prick, his smugness grates, and honestly, he's a little narcissistic.

Much as we hairless-monkeys might like to think of ourselves as perfect, we are far from it. And if we want our readers to connect with our fiction, it needs to be relatable in some way. Which is why it's such a problem when characters are perfect—especially heroes, but that's another book entirely.

And for clarity, when people usually say that's another book, they usually mean it's one they've not written but probably should somewhere off in the metaphorical distance. However, on this occasion, I've already written the other book and it's called *10 Steps to Hero: How to Craft a Kickass Protagonist*.

Perfect people are mirrors. Who wants to look in a mirror and see that they're a bit of a useless fuck up? No one. Yes, we all know we're not perfect, I know I'm a smidge chunkier than I should be—thank you cupcakes and chocolate—I know I'm grumpier than necessary pre-coffee, but that doesn't mean I need reminding, thank you very much. Some of us like to live in absolute denial about our distinct lack of perfection. Which is why a perfect character rolling onto the page is skin-peelingly annoying. Aside from their irritating natures, it's also boring and unrealistic.

But there's one sin greater than all mentioned thus far. If your characters are perfect...

Leans in

Raises eyebrow

How *exactly* do you propose to create any conflict? Perfect characters have nothing to argue or fight over. They're simply perfect. The perfect, dutiful team of bandits and warriors who never get caught.

Clears throat

Bellows

"BOOOORING."

Don't let your characters Robin Hood their way through life and always save the dame and her children's children's children. Where are the flawed opinions? Where's the assholic behavior for other characters to call out and argue over? Give all your characters, side, hero or villain alike, foibles and flaws. Let them fuck up and make mistakes—they're much more appealing that way.

Let's look at some side characters and their flaws. Our dear friend Russell from the movie *Up*, is helpful, yes. But he's persistent to the point of being mildly irritating, bless his cotton socks.

Hermione is bright and clever and helpful, but also has an ego the size of Jupiter which can irk the other characters. Neither of these guys are perfect and your side characters shouldn't be either.

In terms of choosing the flaws, you have two options that will yield maximum impact on the story.

- Pick a trait that's going to irritate the other characters and cause conflict.
- Pick a flaw that's going to be helpful for defeating obstacles.

Didn't Wanna Be Friends Anyway

Alongside banishing perfect characters should be banishing the "must be likable" myth. I'm going to say this once but with force:

Characters don't need to be likable, they need to be interesting.

There's much more power in an interesting character than a likeable one. For example, Sherlock Holmes is arguably one of the most famous and revered characters in history, and yet, if we're honest, he's a bit of a dick. He's abrupt and handles social situations terribly. He's a drug addict and yet he's also loved and adored by millions. Why? Because he's deeply interesting, fascinating, intelligent and he has some redeeming qualities. He's the best at what he does and therefore he's fun to observe.

He's trying to do good, solve crimes and he's on the hero side of the moral line. Which endears him to the reader in spite of his flaws.

Do the same for your side characters.

Flaws are humanizing. They make the larger-than-life characters seem more human. They appeal to our dark sides, to our own flaws and that makes the reader connect with the character more than any likable trait you create.

Making the Unlikeable Appealing

I'm often asked how you make unlikeable characters

likable. Of course, it's easier with a protagonist, you have 400 pages or so of time to make them sympathetic. But with side characters you have considerably less time. What, then, can you do to make an unlikeable character appealing?

There are a few things we can do and we're going to explore each of them in turn.

Positive Trait

Of course, as much as you need a negative trait, you need positive ones too. Hermione is helpful, so is Russell as it happens. Morpheus though, is rigidly determined and steadfast in his faith. This balance in positive and negative traits serves to create a balanced character. Despite flaws, there's good in each of these guys and that is appealing to the reader.

Relatable Wound

Your major side characters will likely have the chance to share some of their history and backstory. Which means they may well have their wound on display. These wounds create a sense of reality because we all have flaws and can understand those fundamental emotions like loss and grief or loyalty and jealousy. This—no matter the character's flaw—creates a connection with the reader because we've all been there and gotten the t-shirts.

Moral Lines

If you have a character that's morally dubious, like Deadpool, but they're always doing bad things for the right reasons, it excuses their behavior. When someone makes a bad decision, if it was because they thought they were helping another human, then as humans we can understand their decisions and it makes their errors understandable if not relatable. We've all made those mistakes, thinking we're helping someone and actually we're just fucking up a bit more. It happens, it's a shitter but we made the decision innocently enough.

Dexter from the TV show and book series is a psychopath who murders people all while working on a police force. However, he only murders people who follow a strict code— such as those who have escaped the police force's law enforcement. He might kill people, but he's doing it for the right reasons. You can use this moralistic balance to carve out likability.

Expertise

If your characters are brilliant at something it makes them more appealing, particularly when they use that expertise to good effect and to help the other characters. In *Six of Crows* by Leigh Bardugo, Inej works for Kaz Brekker. She has the ability to move in silence and frequently uses it to help or support Kaz —even if that means holding a knife to people's throats. While her action is bad, her expertise is what helps and saves Kaz.

Hermione's expertise in spells and knowledge is what helps the team escape trouble over and over again. And so, these repeated acts of "good" endear us to the characters despite their naughty extracurricular activities.

Duty and Kindness

Showing a character caring for another who is smaller or weaker than them in some respect will help to show their humanity. If you want to add a power punch to that, then show your side character caring for another out of *duty*, not out of their caring nature. When someone cares for another out of duty (even when their unlikeable side may not want to do it) it shows that they have a moral compass, and that there is some-thing redeemable about them.

Even though Buzz Lightyear is blind to the reality that he's a toy, it's because he's stoically dedicated to his space force that we forgive the irritation of his naivety.

Change

Another mechanism for making the unlikable taste like sugar and spice is to ensure you show that your side characters can change. See, it's one thing to be a narcissistic testicle wipe, but we humans have soft hearts. If we even sniff the possibility of growth and change, if we think you *might* change, then we can excuse your cutting insults, asshole tendencies and narcis-sism. What we cannot forgive, though, is an unlikeable char-acter who has no room for change.

The nifty thing about this is, it doesn't matter if the char-acter does or does not change. What matters is that they have the *capacity* to. Perhaps like the antihero, rather than changing their flaws, they merely make better decisions, or perhaps they choose not to change but make a sacrifice that saves the dame. Like Hermione who sucks up her pride, or Buzz Lightyear who gives up his belief that the space rangers are real.

3.3 VAGINAS, BIRTHS, AND ORIGIN STORIES

Anyone who's pushed a baby out—a real one, not a book—from their loins knows that child birth is a vajayjay (or belly) massacre. But massacre aside, doesn't that make a vagina powerful? It brings forth into the world an entirely new human: a living, breathing, fleshy skin sack with a beating heart and a brain capable of birthing books and space rockets and marmite and mind-boggling inventions.

Why am I talking of netherly regions and birthing canals in a book about characters? Well, of all the moms I've met, I've never heard two birth stories the same. Every single birth story is unique. These moms have fascinating stories and your side character's origin stories should be too.

Before we continue, let me be clear that not every side character needs an origin story. If your protagonist is checking into a hotel and speaking to the receptionist for all of 3.8 milliseconds, you clearly do not need an origin story. Origin stories are reserved for major side characters only*.

If your side character is a POV character then you're going to want to have their origin or backstory included. Is your side character part of your hero's motley crew? Are they one of her best friends? Perhaps a mentor. Then they're going to get a shit ton of page time, which means you have room for an origin story.

Where's the line? That's a hard one, you have to decide how influential the character is on both your protagonist and the story.

*only being more or less because... rules...

What Is an Origin Story?

An origin story simply explains how a character came to be that character. This isn't a mom boinked dad and nine months later hey presto, Batman's Robin lives.

Take Doc Hudson from the Disney movie *Cars*. His origin story goes something like this: was a famous racing car for years, best of the best, until he has an accident and is forgotten by the world. That's a précis of his origin. But in the film, you get more of the character's backstory, like how he won three Piston Cups, how he created new race moves. He keeps a reminder of his wound in the form of a newspaper article and his old cups. Something that tangles him up with the protagonist's story—where Doc becomes McQueen's coach.

The importance of an origin story for a side character is to explain what fundamental parts of their history has shaped them into the character they are today. You need to include whatever wound or flaw is most salient for that character.

Are they afraid of losing people they love? Then who did they lose in their past? Maybe they didn't lose anyone but were responsible for almost losing a loved one.

What's Included?

Side characters can't have as much exploration as the protagonist, which is why you should only include the historical aspects that have the greatest impact on the character, protagonist, or plot in the present. You can leave the vast majority of the origin stories in your notes files. The important parts are those that have an influence on the story and characters in the now. By now I mean the "present" of your novel. If your character is afraid of dogs because he was bitten by one as a kid but your book's set in space where there are no dogs, it's not bleeding relevant.

If, however, a rabid space dog pops into their craft full of zombie aliens and the only way to freedom is to pass the aforementioned rabid dog to breach the room containing the zombie-killing-weapon-of-amazement, then it's pretty damn relevant.

It's all about the context darling.

Purpose of Origin Stories

Now this bit is really important. There are a couple of key purposes for having an origin story and if you're not hitting all or at least some of them then your character probably doesn't need one.

Purpose 1: To show why your character needs to change

This means your side character needs to be significant enough to the story that they have a change arc aka a major side character. Rather than telling the reader your side character has to change, you can show their need to change through their flawed behavior. This helps to emphasize the character's journey and the change from where they were to where they are now.

Purpose 2: Explain the traits they're displaying in your current story

An origin story will inevitably explain the reasonings behind why your current character behaves the way they do. If your character is an arrogant dick, but in their past they were bullied and crushed by popular kids, you as the reader can understand why they've gone to the other end of the spectrum to compensate for their history. Thus, you're showing the reader the reason for their actions without stating "the bullied becomes the bully."

Purpose 3: To create consequences

If you have an origin story, then you need to ensure that whatever happened in it has an identifiable consequence in the "present" of the plot. If your character has nothing interesting about their origins or their history then don't include it. Chances are they don't need to change and therefore don't have a character arc, thus, leave it out, baby.

An origin story must, must, must have a consequence and that consequence needs to be playing out in the current story.

Origin Story Mistakes

There are some common mistakes with origin stories:

1. Giving too much space to a side character origin story
2. Making the origin story about the character's past instead of the present in the current story
3. Opening your book with the origin story or dropping it early on

Let's go through each of these in turn.

The most important origin story in your novel is your hero's (and/or your villain's). This means their stories get the most page time. For your other side characters, a short flash back, a small conversation, a recollection from the protagonist is more than enough to link past to present.

It's a common mistake to think a character's origin story is only about the past. I mean, after all, this is how the kid got fucked up in the first place, right?

WRONG.

Yes, an origin story covers the creation of a character, but don't forget, the reader is in the present time of your story and nothing should be talked about in the current story unless it's highly relevant.

What this means is that you need to consider *how* it's relevant to your story in the present time. How does the wound created in the past affect the character in the present? What is it stopping him doing? Or how is it impacting his judgment? These are the questions you need to consider.

Jay Asher's *Thirteen Reasons Why* is a fantastic example of how to create origin stories that impact the current plot—and I'm only referencing the first season of the Netflix show which is loyal to the book plot. Hannah, the love interest, kills herself and leaves a set of 13 tapes, each one a sort of origin story for another side character. Each tape is an explanation of how one side character hurt her and the culmination of all those events led to her killing herself. But the point is that each tape, while it explores the past, is highly relevant to the current plot in which Clay Jensen, the protagonist, is trying to find out what happened to Hannah. He uses the origin story tapes to investigate each character she references. It's a masterpiece in origin stories and even if you don't enjoy contemporary YA, I recommend you read the book and then watch the first series just to examine his effective use of origin stories.

Another common mistake is to assume you need to drop your side character's (or protagonist's) origin stories in at the start of your book because chronologically, that's the closest point to it having occurred. This is a mistake of the highest proportion. Yes, it might explain some of your character's current behaviors, but the reader doesn't need you to do that.

Let me explain...

Origin Crumbs

Origin stories should be fed in, alluded to and augmented through the purposeful dropping of breadcrumbs. Why? Because this makes the payoff that much better. For example, the below could be one way you structure it (note this is merely a suggestion, a sprinkling of possibility, not the only way to do it).

- Start with the result of the origin story. What flawed behaviors or poor judgment has the origin story created? Show that first. For example, let's say a side character is scared of boats—have his friends chilling near a lake and the protagonist trying to encourage him onto a jet ski but he's super reluctant and leaves to go home instead, after snapping at the protagonist.
- Then have the protagonist make a reference to "that event" that caused all the problems. Give JUST enough detail that the reader can label or identify the event in connection with the side character who's stormed off. Like referring to it as "the lake incident." This label gives it meaning and importance and makes the name a reference point for the reader and other characters. It makes it super recognizable when it comes up again later and last, it's foreshadowing because no event that's shrouded in mystery stays that way for long.
- If this were the protagonist's origin story you could

loop the above two scenarios a couple of times. But as a side character that's probably the most you're going to get before the protagonist then calls them out and discusses the original event. Be sure to include a reference, flashback, or discussion about the lake incident, explaining what happened.

- Last, you need to show the side character overcoming the wound and getting on the lake later in the story.

Creating Origin Stories

If you're unsure how to create an origin story, here are some questions you can base your thinking around:

- What were the most significant events in your character's past?
- Are there any painful or overly happy memories?
- Who or what influenced the character?
- What kind of home or background does your character come from?
- If you had to pick one emotion to summarize the character's childhood, what would it be?

3.4 BACKSTORY, FLASHBACKS, AND MEMORIES

Flashbacks are used for a variety of reasons, they're like milk-shakes—multiple flavors exist. The standard flashback is used as a tool to reveal something about a character's backstory, and in doing so, reveal something to the reader or the character themselves via reflection. In other words, the past helps make sense of the present.

But more than that, flashbacks can be used to play with time and the reader's sense of order and chronology. Last, they're a promise, for example, when a scene starts with a disaster and the clock winds backward a few weeks to show the events that run up to it—like the start of *Deadpool* the movie—it makes a promise to the reader that no matter how much it looks like everything is going swimmingly, the hero will end up in the shitstorm disaster they read at the start of the chapter.

Flashy Ups, Flashy Downs

There are a number of benefits to using flashbacks, but they have a slathering of issues too. Let's look at the downsides first:

- By definition, they're already over. So, no matter what negative thing happens, the reader will know the hero survives, or at least for now. It makes it a bit of a spoiler.
- Flashbacks slow the pace of the story and disrupt the narrative flow because you flip the reader out of the current action and plot and into the past.
- On top of slowing the pace, it also lacks immediacy and connection with the reader because it happened so long ago

Alright, nuff negativity, what are the benefits?

- First up, it's like a dollop of motive cake. Past events shape us, and in showing key events to the reader, it can provide solid justifications and reasons for why your character behaves the way they do.
- It can explain the lead up to an event and the reasons why a character is in the shit-suation they're in

What Flashbacks Do You Include?

The most fundamental point about a flashback is that it needs to serve a purpose. Examples of some purposes include:

- Driving the plot forward by motivating, inspiring, or demotivating the protagonist
- Reveal information or a secret that helps or hinders the protagonist
- Deepen characterization of either the protagonist or the side character
- Deepen the emotional connection with the reader

How do you tell which flashbacks to paint in a glorious fit of rainbow color and which to bury under the porch with the bodies? Well, if it doesn't serve one of the above purposes or another very clear purpose, then ditch it.

But if it does, then free feel to lube up and slide that bad boy in. Below are some questions that might help you to decide what flashbacks to pick or provide prompts to help you form the flashbacks.

- What is it about this side character's past that makes her memorable?
- What events in their history had the biggest impact or changed your side character?
- In these events, what were the key moments?
- How are these relevant to the current plot and action?
- What one event in the side character's past links to the theme?
- How have those events shaped and warped your character's viewpoints because of those events?

A Duo of Structural Necessity

Before we all strip naked and dance in a shower of flashbacks, a word of caution—err on the side of having your flashbacks later rather than sooner. Yes, many prologues are flashbacks but a prologue does what a prologue does. If you start your novel in the past in a flashback it's disorienting to the reader who will then spend the next 300 pages in the present with the protagonist in their current state. Rather than setting your reader up with one set of historical expectations and then a scene or two later forcing them to reorient, it's much better to allow the reader to get to know the protagonist and side characters and then show them the past. Does that mean you can never do it? No, course not. There are always exceptions, but as a guide, it's more effective to establish all of your characters in their current story world before you throw the reader back.

Second, if you've read *The Anatomy of Prose*, you'll know all about the importance of scene anchoring. But it's absolutely crucial with a flashback. The reader will be thrown from what they know and the world you've created into an entirely new time and place. Therefore, you need to orient them and drop specific details explaining, describing and defining this new world. Specifically, the time, place and POV.

One bonus tip for structuring a flashback is to use a trigger. Let's say your side character picks up a key. The key reminds the protagonist of an event in their past when someone handed them a key and disaster struck. The trigger to move into the flashback is the key, and you can use the same trigger to get out of the flashback and signal to the reader the scene is over. For example:

I walked into the room as Sandy handed a key to Brandon. Iron rust flaked off the stem and floated to the floor. [entry trigger] I recognized that key.

The last time she gave Brandon that key was the day Danny died. She'd handed it over, smooth and shiny with newness, and all three of us went to the barn to finish Danny's new cot. We'd sanded and nailed the wooden crib for hours. Every rivet and bar were perfect. As the sun set, a breeze rippled through the barn door, dragging dust balls, dead leaves and plant detritus inside. A shriek, hollow and sharp, tore through the air. My skin crawled. Brandon froze. It was the kind of cry that cut scars into your memories.

I glanced at the key in Brandon's hand, [exit trigger] an antique now, but the screams were just as fresh.

Flashbacks and Side Characters

But what good are flashbacks when a flashback is for the main character? It's true, the only characters who should get full scene, immersive flashbacks from their past are the protagonist or main POV character. But as we saw in the last section, flashbacks are a useful tool to reveal the why's and how's behind a character's wounds and flaws, as well as the reasonings for their current behaviors. Which is why they're useful for side characters. A flashback is usually a lengthy section, often an entire scene. Of course, you can have minor references to past occurrences, or paragraphs like the above example, but a flashback in its purest form is closer to a full scene.

How then do flashbacks help a side character? You can bend the protagonists-only-have-flashback rules, be sly, use a flashback to your advantage.

Let's say your protagonist is recalling the night their sister died, perhaps his best friend (now) was his best friend (then). Why not draw the bestie into that flashback, show the side character and his reactions, how he helped the protagonist, and the role he played that night? This can illuminate the history of that side character and reveal something about their personality as well as serving the main purpose of illuminating the protagonist's wound origin.

But what if your side character wasn't present? What if you still want to show a flashback but from their perspective? This is a fine balance. If your side character has a narrative POV then you have more wiggle room to do this, you can just move into their perspective and show the flashback. However, for those characters who aren't lucky enough to be a POV character, the story is someone else's, so you can't go dumping eight decades of their history into the plot. Equally, you need depth. To avoid pancake characters, you're going to have to add *something* of their backstory. The art is in the balance. Here are some ways to do that:

- Short flashbacks—use triggers to initiate a short paragraph flashback. Like "old" banter phrases or seeing a photograph or an item that jogs a memory
- Protagonists reference a short memory about the side character (make sure it's relevant to the plot though)
- Memories discussed in dialogue

Here's a short snippet from a draft of *The Scent of Death*, the novel I'm currently working on:

Frank shakes his head, just once. His gel-hard hair doesn't budge an inch. Then he lays down on the roof of his Chevy, sucking in a deep puff of his cigar. It makes his ridiculous-attempt-at-a-mustache twitch as he holds the stogie between his teeth and blows the smoke out around the sides. I suppress an eye roll. Frank swears he doesn't model himself on *Don Corleone* but to everyone else he's the perfect pinup of a 1940s mafia lovechild. He's been like that since the night we snuck into his dad's cinema room and watched *The Godfather*. Neither of us actually gave a toss about the film, we only wanted to watch it because it was rated 18 and we were 13. Frank nicked the dregs of a bottle of whiskey his dad had stashed in one of his office cabinets and I'd saved up for some microwave popcorn. I still remember Frank looking like a right zombie; his eyes were as wide as testicles the entire movie. Next day he wore a waistcoat, didn't he? Thinking about it, I ain't seen him without one since.

Yes, this is a flashback of sorts, but it's not a full scene. We don't see the ins and outs of that entire evening, the events of that night don't push the plot forward, but they do deepen the characterization of Frank. They tell the reader something. It's a small, paragraph-length look at a memory of the protagonist to help deepen the characterization of a side character. It's just enough in this scene to add a bit of flavor without a full-blown tangential side scene led by a side character. Of course, you can use this technique multiple times in a novel to deepen a range of characters, for worldbuilding and myriad other uses.

You can get the side characters checklist to help you craft flashbacks into your stories by visiting: sachablack. co.uk/sidecharacters

3.5 COOEY, IT'S ME!

Try not to shudder, but I want you to imagine walking into a room full of new people. Societal norms dictate that we introduce ourselves. We make sweeping glances around the room to establish the unwritten power and hierarchy in the room, perhaps raise a judgmental eyebrow at what he's wearing or the odd-shaped bulge in his pants, and then we make our rounds.

It's the same for your characters. When the reader first stumbles upon your characters it's vitally important you introduce them. They want to judge and raise eyebrows and understand what the character looks like. The problem with not introducing your characters is that just like writers, readers will make shit up. Perhaps they'll decide your basic white girl looks more like an oldy worldy duchess from some long-forgotten aristocracy, or give her goggly green eyes and a piglet-shaped nose, or lord knows what other random visual delicacy.

You as the creator might know every orifice and intimate lip measurement of your characters, but your readers—when they first pick up your book—know sweet fuck all. You need to decide what the priority is for a character's introduction and it's not always the obvious eye color and aesthetics.

That said, how your character looks should tell the reader about their personality without sledgehammering them in the face. Consider what part of their physical appearance you *need* the reader to know about. Is there a part of their *physical* personality that tells the reader about their *psychological* personality or something about their inner core? If so, that should be your priority for description. Don't describe his bitch stare unless there's a catch—do the bitch stares get him caught later? Is he unable to disguise himself? Does his bitch stare make someone fall in love with him? Your focus in a character's first entrance has to be whatever is most important about their personality or the attributes that make your character most unique. Appearances can give insight into the character's life, personality, and self-image. If she has a dancer's build, she's probably a dancer. Or perhaps more mysteriously she has a dancers build but *isn't* dancing. There's a whole story that needs unravelling just in her build. It creates a "why" question. If a character has soil under his nails, he's either a gardener or he's been burying body parts.

On Appearance Details and Voice

The very first line of V.E. Schwab's *A Darker Shade of Magic* goes like this:

> "Kell wore a very peculiar coat. It had neither one side, which would be conventional, nor two, which would be unexpected, but *several*, which was, of course, impossible."

Schwab then continues for another paragraph describing this coat. It's a key part of Kell's personality and he's never seen without it. So of course, this is the priority when he's described. It's not until later that we find out more detail about his appearance—like the fact his eyes are different colors.

What do you want readers to focus on? What do you want readers to know about your characters? See, it's not just the items of clothing or aspects of physical appearance you choose to describe that's important, it's the voice you choose to describe them in that helps shape their personality too.

Let's talk about active description for a sec...

Active Description and Subtext

Active Description describes two types of description. The first occurs when you create descriptions in the voice of your character or narrator and not your voice as the author. Second —and this is often but not always a result of the first point— when you make your descriptions work twice for you, once on the surface describing the physicality of whatever you're describing and then secondly through subtext. I'll give you examples of this below, but first let's just clarify what we mean by subtext:

Subtext: If text is the blood-stained ink you scrawl on the page, aka the physical words your reader sees, then subtext is everything else. Everything you haven't said but your reader infers anyway. Subtext is the meaning between the lines. It's the message your readers take from a scene without you explicitly telling them.

You know when you're disagreeing and your partner says "I'm fine" and yet you know they are anything *but* fine! That... That is a glorious shining example of subtext.

When you engage active description effectively, you also employ subtext. Take Schwab's description above. She could have said this:

Example 1: Kell wore a weird coat.

But what would that have told us? Fuck nothing apart from

the fact a character called Kell owned an unusual coat. Well, fine. But the reader doesn't get to know the character, they don't get to dive into their psyche and they don't get to hear the character's voice. Thankfully, that's not what Schwab did. Let's break the sentence down and see what she actually did using active description, subtext and making everything work for her more than once.

"Kell wore a very peculiar coat. *[Schwab is careful to choose just the right word "peculiar" to describe this coat. It's an unusual and textured word. It's more powerful and unique than "weird" or "odd" and tells us that Kell is proud of this coat because you don't choose "peculiar" unless you understand the impact you're going to have.]* It had neither one side, which would be conventional, *[The choice of the word "conventional" tells the reader that the voice narrating is intellectual, and again "conventional" is juxtaposed against "peculiar", thus reinforcing the strangeness of Kell and his coat]* nor two, which would be unexpected, but *several*, which was, of course, impossible." *[Here the use of the word impossible hints at the magic to come. It promises the reader that something magical and fantastic is coming because something that cannot possibly exist, does. Thus, it must be magic. This is subtext. Schwab hasn't told us that the coat is magical, she's only told us that it's impossible. It's our imagination that does the rest of the work for us.]*

Introducing Voice

Another factor you want to consider when introducing your characters is the fact that the first time we meet them is also the first time we're going to hear their voice. It's important you give their voice maximum "voiciness." Let's look at how Schwab did that in the above quote. She used punctuation and cadence to enhance the voice. In example 1, the one I butchered, the cadence is flat and telling and because of that, you cannot *hear* a voice be it narrator, character, author or otherwise.

But in the original Schwab version, she's used punctuation, repetition and additional narrational interjections such as "which would be conventional," and "which would be unexpected" to add to the narrator's voice. She also uses the "which would be" repetitive phrasing to enhance voice through rhythm and the repetition breeds familiarity. The narrator doesn't *have* to add these reflections but doing so augments their sound, gives it a clear style and flare, something that on introduction helps the reader to form an opinion about them.

Let's look at the sentence if we remove the voice:

> **Example 2:** Kell wore a very peculiar coat. It had neither one side, nor two, but *several.*

The narrator's voice is lost completely. There is a little more voice than in example 1, but only just. Schwab's narrator is voiciest in the additional reflections and natural repetition that we all do when enthused about something. In this case, the coat. What this does is really draw the reader in. Subconsciously we start to know and understand the narrator and gain some familiarity with them. While most narrators are protagonists, all of this applies to side characters who are narrating or who are point of view characters too.

Testicle Ears and Nipple Eyes

Okay back to physical descriptions. We know that your side characters don't—and shouldn't—get as much page time as your hero. But that means you need to do more in the short time you have to create the same sense of character depth as your protagonist's introduction.

One way of making your characters "pop" is to make them

visually "stand out." Now, **let me caveat this heavily.** That doesn't mean making them have testicles for ears or nipples for eyes. And it certainly doesn't mean stigmatizing a sector of society for the sake of ticking a box, and finally, it doesn't mean creating overtly "token" characters either. It means thinking outside the box for your characters.

Kell is introduced to the audience via his jacket—a highly unusual jacket. The jacket changes its look and shape and it's something Kell wears permanently. It's unexpected, unusual and that makes it—and him—stand out.

It's a tiny detail, but one that is memorable because of its unusualness and it hasn't got anything to do with his skin color, his sexuality, or his able-bodiedness.

Think outside the box. Here are some ideas:

- Does your side character have a special weapon?
- Do they wear a particular type of make up?
- Do they have an unusual dress sense?
- Do they smell a particular way?
- Do they have a special item they always carry?
- Do they smoke?
- Do they wear odd shoes?
- Do they carry a piece of kit?
- Is their hair dyed?
- Have they got a specific sense of humor?

If your side character's voice doesn't match his appearance, then that's probably what should be mentioned. If she has a birth mark in the shape of a screwdriver on her neck, that might need to be something to focus on.

There are a thousand different ways you can create unique identifiers for your characters without stigmas attached, all it takes is a little thought outside the box.

Cooey, it's Still ME!

Characters need to be "introduced" multiple times. I use quotes because it's not as straightforward as literally repeating the character's name and description.

Why do you need to introduce them more than once?

Well, first of all, you as the author will know your world and your story better than any other reader, editor, or mega fan will ever know it. You literally created it from the mass of gray cells and squidge in your brain. No one can know your world as intimately as you.

Second, readers forget. Humans forget, hell, who hasn't gotten a character name wrong or made someone have brown hair instead of blonde? I'll be honest, as a voracious reader myself, unless your characters stand out, they'll blur into the mass of things I've read. I will forget which character had the teddy bear fetish or what flavor of kinky tattoo was on the love interest's penis. Actually, that's not true, if your character has a penis tattoo, I'm going to remember. But you get my point.

Chekov's Gun

Another reason for needing deepening description is because if you want to highlight a particular feature, you can by manipulating what the reader sees or doesn't see.

Think about Chekov's gun. The reader may brush over the detail when the gun is described in a scene, but you can be assured that once that gun goes missing, they'll notice. What's missing is often more salient than what's not. If, for example, Kell suddenly lost his jacket, the reader would notice, it would mean something.

Deepening Description

Okay, we know they need to be described more than once, but...*pulls up giant megaphone* that does not mean you need to introduce the exact same aspects of a character with the exact same description. Being told a character has blue eyes four times is repetitive and dull and it doesn't deepen the description. You can describe the eye color repeatedly but each time with a different meaning or aspect highlighted. Likewise, another mistake to avoid is creating huge great sweeping paragraphs of description all about your character's physical appearance.

Pick one, two or maybe at a push three salient aspects of your character and the aspects that will work doubly hard for you and you stick to those, you can cover other aspects as the story progresses to deepen your characterization.

Thus, your challenge with each successive entrance is to deepen the characterization by finding new ways to describe features or layer meanings and connections to those features. Go further into their personality, make the descriptions worker harder, smarter, reveal more. Let's look at an example:

Entrance 1: Charles stood tall and straight, never able to shrug his soldier training off, even on his vacation days. He glanced at me; his blue eyes cold as they locked on mine.

Entrance 2: I always thought Charles's eyes were everyday blue. Now I see they're much more than that. He might have stood tall and rigid, but he couldn't make his eyes lie. They whispered too many secrets in gazes and angles. His eyes wore a coat of deep ocean that day, as if bubbling under the waves and eddies were plans and ideas and maybe, just maybe, a little piece of hope.

Entrance 3: Stella left and the instant the door clicked shut, Charles's stiff posture crumpled, his shoulders sagged, his navy-blue uniform wrinkled as he slumped in the armchair.

Here we have three different interactions with a character: Charles. Rather than mentioning the same blue eyes and the fact he was a soldier every single time, we receive the information in entrance one and then dig deeper into it in entrance two and three. In two, we explore his eye color and posture further, rather than repeating the fact they're blue, we've used his eyes to explore other aspects and consequences of the blue. His eyes tell us he hides his emotions, he doesn't want whatever he's feeling exposed. But equally, the reader can infer that no matter how much Charles might try to keep his emotions hidden, the protagonist and thus the reader can tell he's suppressing feelings.

In entrance three, we see a whole new level of depth to Charles's character. First up, we know that to date, Charles has always remained stoic, soldier-like and stiff in his manner. Yet, in this scene, we see that crumble and he exposes his vulnerabilities. Charles's baseline is stiff and emotionless, but every character will break eventually, no human or character stays on their baseline of emotion. That's why this deepens his characterization, because we see and infer that Stella—for whatever reason—has the ability to get under his skin. We're not told this directly in the text, but shown through Charles's body language and obvious relief at her exit. The uniform rumpling is symbolic and representative of his emotional state too, a juxtaposition against his normally stiff, straight manner—again, another unsaid but visual clue to the subtext of what's going on there.

Be intentional with both your introductions and the elements you choose to describe to make them work double for you.

3.6 CLOAKS, DAGGERS, AND SURPRISES

Many writers think that cloaks and daggers are a great method for creating tension. But there's a difference between puffing smoke in your reader's face and actually creating an air of mystery. What doesn't create an air of mystery is skipping side character details. See, leaving out details just confuses the reader and leaves them feeling like your story is less "mystery" and more vague nothingness.

Alas, dear writers, creating an air of mystery around a character doesn't mean intentionally missing out key information about their personality or background. There's no mystery in having a character with zero depth or background. Mystery instead comes from unanswered questions, details that don't add up, from knowing a character holds information you don't have, and the contradictions that play out between. Mystery is actually created when you push the reader to guess and surmise. What you need to do is get the reader to speculate about what's going on, to ask themselves who the hell is that character and what on earth she meant when she said that.

Leaving out detail about your side characters just creates 2D characters that fall flat for the reader. How do you fix it?

Contradictions, Opinions, Secrets, and Shade

First up, contradictions work a treat. Rather than bringing in a new side character and allowing everything to add up perfectly, make 2+2=5. Perhaps a character gets a crucial date wrong, or maybe they say they were in one place during a murder, and then in another scene they claim to have been somewhere else. These lies rub up against each other and cause friction, they make the reader disbelieve the character but without answers and without knowing the truth. The more contradictions you throw, the more mysterious the character becomes. Like all good things, moderation is key; throw in too many contradictions and suddenly the character becomes unbelievable. A couple spread out over the course of the story are enough to tantalize the reader.

You can reveal information in the story without having your protagonist put two and two together too. This is a great trick to let your reader in on the answer without having your protagonist figure it out... yet.

Drag the clues and subsequent reveals out over multiple scenes. Leave a breadcrumb trail of details, never enough in one scene to reveal the answer, just enough that shit doesn't add up, and more important than anything, don't reveal the answer to a dropped breadcrumb in the next scene. Leave the reader hanging for a couple or hell, a dozen scenes. It's a drug, they'll smother their eyeballs over your pages, dribbling and salivating like the filthy addicts they are. I'm clearly not speaking from experience, ahem.

Another trick is to use the protagonist's opinion and fears to influence the reader. If the protagonist surmises a side character is suspicious, the chances are, the reader may agree. Or, better yet, they may disagree entirely.

Secrets and lies are another fabulous tool for creating an air of mystery. See section 8.2 for more information on how to use secrets. One last trick is to have characters with flaws, foibles, and negative traits; when they're unlikable it creates distance between the character and the reader, meaning you're more easily able to manipulate what the reader sees and takes note of.

Contradictions and Surprises

Some of the most interesting side characters are those that are surprising. How do you create surprising characters? Well, aside from marrying an array of contradictions together, you can do something unexpected.

When something unexpected happens, it shocks our system. It sends a burst of adrenaline around our bodies. Our autonomic system kicks in and we're on alert to fight, flight, or freeze. We're evolutionarily evolved to pay attention to surprises. If you can subvert the expected, your reader will sit up and take note. What does this look like in a story?

- Reactions that are unexpected or out of character or the opposite of how they've previously behaved
- Plot twists
- Reveals

Kato, one of the side characters in my YA fantasy series has been likened to puppies and sunshine. He's loving, kind, and a bit of a diva. When I wrote a scene where he meets his mother —who abandoned him when he was a child for...reasons—I expected him to be emotional and upset. Readers would expect that too because it's in character. It matches their expectations. But the scene didn't work. I changed it around and had him angry and cross with her, and guess what? The scene was far more shocking and emotional because he reacted more authentically.

Just because you craft characters to be one way for the majority of the time, say, kind and tolerant, doesn't mean they have to be that way or feel that way for the entire story. It's much more realistic to expect them to lash out and react when an intensely emotional event occurs. This is natural emotional modulation and it's something to consider with your side characters.

If your side character has been a pillar of stoicism, then a fleeting outburst is always a dramatic show of realism. We don't feel one emotion for all of eternity. No, we feel a multitude of things, though a word of caution here. Humans, generally, are creatures of habit and it's in these habits that we create personality and "character." I appreciate this sounds conflicting, so to summarize: ensuring your characters have emotional consistency for the vast majority of your book is key to creating realistic characterization. However, what is also "real" is the occasional emotional outburst or breakdown—we are, after all, only human. This will help to create an air of "oh, perhaps we didn't know that character so well after all." It's depth and mystery for your reader. Note though, that I said occasional.

3.7 FUNNY FUCKERS

If they're not naturally funny, then writers often say "humor" is something they avoid in their stories. But I'm here to banish the fear and encourage you to sprinkle a liberal dose of funny fucker over your manuscript.

Sense of Humor

For me personally, sense of humor is one of the most important factors in my friends and loved ones. I love laughing, taking the piss out of myself and engaging in loving banter. My wife has the driest sense of humor of anyone I've ever met. She makes Jack Dee look like a cheerleader. In fact, she's so dry that I spend a solid portion of my time trying to translate, apologize or explain her humor through stifled laughter before anyone is mortally offended.

Humor, though, is one of the areas of character creations writers shy away from. The mythical nature of humor occurs because if a joke doesn't land, it has the total opposite effect, making the scene clunky and awkward. But fear not, my beauties, humor isn't the scary awkward nasty you think it is.

First up, one of the best ways to confront humor is to actually look at the many shades of it out there. Like monomouth—a concept from character dialogue (see section 4.5)—many authors give each of their cast members identical senses of humor.

Oof, nay, my pretties. We can do better than that.

It's time to sprinkle a dash of dry, a portion of word-wit, and a dose of puns over your characters, not least because it helps to differentiate and therefore deepen your characterization. Here's a list of ideas to help get you started.

Sarcasm

Sarcasm is usually an ironic or satirical comment sprinkled with a liberal dose of humor, often dished out in one-liners or banter at the expense of another. For example, if someone walks into a room stinking of far too much perfume, a sarcastic fellow might say, "Wow, nice perfume, how long did you marinate in it?" Examples of sarcastic people—yours truly, Dr. Gregory House from *House*, Chandler Bing from *Friends* (see also "Dry Humor" below), Charlie Harper from *Two and a Half Men*, and Howard from the *Big Bang Theory*.

Dry Humor

Dry humor is often called deadpan—it's seen as a typically British style of humor. The main element is the total, complete, and utter lack of emotional expression, tone, or output. A person with a dry sense of humor will say controversial things with a stoically straight face in order to shock and surprise their audience. Examples of people with dry humor include Jack Dee, *Black Adder*, Chandler Bing from *Friends,* John Cleese as Basil Fawlty in *Fawlty Towers,* and Ricky Gervais.

Pun Humor

Puns are a form of word play. They work by playing off the fact words can have double meanings, or from the use of homophones and homographs. In other words, intentionally mixing up the meaning of words because they sound or read the same while having different meanings. These jokes tend to illicit stifled chuckles and eye rolls. Think of a middle-aged dad joke and you're not far off. Personally, I find dad jokes hilarious. However, there's quite a clear line with pun jokes, some will elicit a giggle while others will cause your reader to roll their eyes—always a tricky balancing act.

I hope you're ready for this...

Typical dad joke...

"Dad, did you get a haircut?"
"No, I got them all cut."

ho, ho, ho truly terrible, right? Bet you rolled your eyes and smiled just a teeny bit.

"What do you call cheese that isn't yours?"
"Nacho cheese."

"Why can't a nose be 12 inches?"
"Because then it would be a foot."

I hope you can hear my cackle and snorts as I write these up. If you're not at least smirking, get out. Off with your head. I demand at LEAST a lip twitch.

For everyone else, you're welcome.

Self-Deprecating and Empowerment Humor

When you self-deprecate, you belittle yourself, and make yourself the brunt of a joke, by undervaluing or reprimanding yourself in order to get a laugh from your audience. Sometimes, though, this can create the opposite effect, actually empowering both the speaker and the audience, removing stigmas, and enabling a freer environment to discuss and campaign on certain topics.

Comedians who use this humor include Joan Rivers, Woody Allen, Don Knotts, and Jo Brand.

Usually, comedians or characters will base their act around one particular factor in their life, for example "the harassed mom" set.

Another example includes Drew Lynch who appeared in the 2015 *America's Got Talent* show. Drew had an accident while playing softball that damaged his vocal cords and left him with a speech impairment. He then used this impairment to show people how you can turn a negative into a positive and created a comedy set around his impairment and the misunderstandings it can create. Please, though, know that this type of humor is often left to those who can write using "own voices." If you are not part of the sector of society the character comes from, it's better to use more generic topics like "the workaholic" or "the exhausted mum." Go to Google and have a look for memes as typically they use this type of humor. Please don't risk stigmatizing a group of society for a laugh—there are better ways to make your readers smile.

Toilet Humor

Often used in kids' books, or for younger audiences, this kind of humor is situated around poops, wee, gusts of wind from your orifices and other bodily boogers.

Dark Humor

I won't lie, I love a bit of dark humor. I always like to think of dark humor as the kind of joke that elicits a gasp and someone whispering, "oooh, too soon." Dark humor takes dark, depressing, political, or controversial topics and makes light of the situation.

Monty Python Humor

If you've not watched Monty Python then stop whatever you're doing... Wait, you're reading. No, don't stop that. After you've finished the book go watch the Monty Python movies. These guys create completely illogical and absurd situations, which are so nonsense they're hilarious. This silly kind of humor can be used by anyone in any situation.

Slapstick Humor

Slapstick humor is harder to create in a novel because it's such a physical type of comedy—think Laurel and Hardy. That said, you can still recreate perfectly timed mishaps in your book if you have a clumsy character, or perhaps a character who is the exact opposite and the catastrophes are funny because they're embarrassing. Examples include Laurel and Hardy, Mr. Bean, Ty Burrell from *Modern Family* and Charlie Chaplin.

Innuendos

Innuendos are for the crafty, filthy-minded comedians of the world. An innuendo can seem polite and innocent on the surface, but when you dive into the hidden meaning, there's usually something sexual, insulting, derogatory, or rude under the surface. Mostly used as sexual references, the jokes can be as funny as they are eye-roll inducing. An example of an innuendo is as follows:

"I've given up sexual innuendos for Lent... So far it's been pretty hard."

Ba-Dum-Chaaa. Innuendos are often found in kids shows and movies. Now, before you shriek in alarm, remember, innuendos can be read two ways—kiddos, because they're innocent, read them innocently. But for the parents watching, we often cackle silently to ourselves. *The Simpsons* is great at this. Lord Farquaad from *Shrek* is a prime example too. His name, Farquaad, is a nod to "fuckwad".

Sharpness

If you've read this section and your sphincter is still tight at the prospect of having to sprinkle humor into your work, then fear not. There is another way. The foundation of a lot of humor is actually sharpness. Let your characters be quick, if not funny.

3.8 ANCHORING SIDE CHARACTERS

When you have a large cast of characters, one way of making the lesser characters more real and memorable is by anchoring them to something like a location. Before you get uppity and send me emails about why your characters are on an epic quest for a sword and therefore have to traipse through mountains filled with elephant-sized killer fleas and swamps infested with rabid sheep skeletons, it's cool. Don't worry. You can anchor them to other things too. This is just one technique you could use if you want to.

No rules, remember?

Besides, if your characters are on a quest, perhaps the "anchor" you're tying them to is the journey itself, the cart, or a fire every evening. The act of anchoring is more important than the "thing" they're tied to.

Of course, sometimes you need these characters to appear in other locations, and I'm not suggesting they need hand-cuffing to one physical space. I'm saying that intentional, anchored repetition breeds familiarity and that's especially true for side characters who aren't appearing in your stories that often.

If your characters are here, there, and everywhere then it's harder for associations to build up in a reader's mind.

Using Items to Anchor a Character

Hoa, a stone eater, from *Fifth Season,* the first book in the Broken Earth trilogy,* can often be found carrying a bag of rocks. You never see him without it, it's important to him, and the bag of rocks is relevant as the story progresses and we learn it's his source of food. Other anchor items we've mentioned previously, like Sherlock's pipe, Iron Man's suit, and Thor's hammer. Other anchors include Hagrid's umbrella wand, Sajid in the movie *East is East* is *always* in a green bomber jacket, and in Philip Pullman's *Northern Lights*, Lyra and every side character from her world has a daemon. Yes, these daemons are other characters, but they never leave the humans' sides and thus help to anchor the human characters. In *Ocean's Eleven* the movie, Rusty (played by Brad Pitt) is *always* seen eating something in every scene, his anchor is food.

*Which, side note, I highly recommend the Broken Earth trilogy if you want a schooling in how to use second person POV, which Jemisin does masterfully.

Using Emotion to Anchor a Character

This one is a little harder to pin down. But, establishing a baseline emotion can help you deepen character, especially when you then demonstrate them acting out of character. Snape in *Harry Potter,* for example, is always sneering, aggrieved, and resentful of pretty much everything. When he acts out to save Harry, and shows the merest whiff of affection and sacrifices himself for him it is shocking to the core and shows enormous depth of character.

Inside Out, the Disney Pixar movie, is a great example of

how to choose baseline emotions. Each side character *is* an emotion. The movie is set predominantly inside the head of a pre-teen girl, each emotion she feels is a character and that character embodies a range of that emotion's strengths. Anger, for example, is sometimes mildly irked, and sometimes he's so angry he blows his lid and fire burns from his scalp! This range of emotional depth helps to deepen their characterization and is a great lesson on not assuming all emotions are singular in their expression.

Using Location to Deepen Theme in Side Characters

The most frequent form of anchoring for side characters is to use a location. You can also hook location into the theme. For example, one of my side characters in *The Scent of Death*, Frank, is gay and can't bring himself to come out. I could use locational symbolism and draft multiple scenes in a graveyard or hospital or animal sanctuary—some location that's connected to "saving" or not as the case may be. The subtler the symbolism the better of course.

In *Meat Market* written by Juno Dawson, Jana is the protagonist. During the story she has to choose whether or not to stay in college or continue with her modeling career. Sabah is her best friend, and the vast majority of the time, we—the reader— see Sabah in the college, representing one half of the question Jana is facing.

Another reason place is a handy little critter, is because place has purpose. If your character is always in the library, that tells you something about that character. They're studious or a perpetual learner or maybe they're researching for a dastardly plan. Making elements of your novel work twice for you is super handy because it has a third effect, it creates realism and depth. Humans tend to be in a place for a reason. If your side characters have a reason for being somewhere, it shovels boat loads of realism in. Plus, it creates habits which deepens characterization further. Hermione Granger from the *Harry Potter* series is a good example of this, if she's not in a library, then we see her holding books. "Knowledge" is her anchor, be it in the form of a study location or the items she always holds.

3.9 SCENE POWER AND DISPROPORTIONATE PAGE TIME

While none of your characters *have* to be in every scene, your major side characters should be in the vast majority of them. Now, there's a caveat to that, because while it's nice to bring side characters in, you can't have them hanging out in the background sniffing books, and picking their armpits. They actually need to be doing something. Specifically, helping the protagonist to drive the story on. They need to engage in the action else be forgotten by the reader. And yet they can't take over the scene, they can't lead it or drive it or be in control of it.

Let's talk about a concept called "scene power." When you (in realz life) walk into a room, you'll know subconsciously or consciously who wields the power. It's innate for humans and animals alike. Instinctively we know who the pack leader is. But in fiction, although the pack leader should be the protagonist, sometimes we get these pesky side characters that like to steal the limelight. And it's totally natural to veer towards whoever wields the power in the room, whoever commands attention, or charms and romances the audience. Maybe you're the kind to slip in the back door and casually observe from the back. Maybe you're the one twirling the audience around your fingers, or perhaps you're always stood at the right-hand side of that person. We *feel* it. It's like a tangible power in the room. Next time you go to a party, try and purposefully notice who wields the power in any room. It's the same in your books. Regardless of how many characters there are in a scene, one should always be the puppet master, and much as we adore our side characters, it shouldn't be them.

Striking a Balance

One of the most common questions I get around side characters is how do you stop them stealing the limelight? How do you stop them taking over the scene or story and making it about them? The problem is that your protagonist's core circle of sidekicks need to be on the page in order to defend the hero from killer crows, the Kraken's irritable bowels or Voldemort's flights and fancies. But they can't encroach on protagonist territory. How to strike a balance?

There's a key principle you need to adhere to: **side characters can be involved as much as you want, but they can't lead or drive the action.** That pleasure is reserved for the hero. With the decision making or "reactionary" force that leads the gaggle of friends into trouble or towards victory, it's **always driven by the protagonist.** It's the protagonist who makes the decision to lead the group down tunnel A and not B. It's the protagonist who weighs up all the evidence from the crime scene fellow officers. It's the protagonist who gets the epiphany and figures out who killed Karen—though of course, it will have been that last tangential throwaway line from his second-in-command that helped him slot the final puzzle piece into place.

And that's the rub. Side characters feed the protagonist. They help, support, provide information, occasionally find clues. But it's always the protagonist piecing the clues together and using page time to think and reflect, which is why they make the decision to dive into peril and lead the charge.

Let's look at this in practice.

The below is a scene from near the climax of the first book in my YA fantasy series, *Keepers*. This is first person present tense and Eden is the protagonist. Trey, Kato, Bo, and Cassian are all side characters. I've edited this excerpt to purposefully let the side characters take over. Note that this will be difficult to read because there's no driving protagonist; stick with it, I'll explain how to fix it after:

Kato slices Bo's palm, and smears the blood over the dagger.

Cassian stands up, walks to the window, and gazes at the courtyard below. "We don't have a plan. You need a plan before a fight."

"Is that cage fighting wisdom?" Kato growls.

Cassian glances at him; if he notices the irritation in his voice, he doesn't seem bothered by it.

"It's logic," he says, turning to me. "You were lucky Maddison and Arden were there when he attacked last time. This time we're on our own."

"Maybe," I say, hoping Arden and Hermia got my messages.

"But he's right—we do need a plan," Trey says.

Kato finishes bandaging Bo's hand then slumps into the seat next to her and strokes her head.

"Well, Victor was wounded by Arden. So, he won't come on his own, which means he'll bring wolves, and wolves always hunt in packs," I say.

"And they always isolate their prey," Trey adds.

"Right," I nod.

"So, we need bait. I guess that's Eden," Kato says.

"No. We need Eden to use the knife on Victor. If one of the

wolves gets her before she gets to Victor we're all screwed. I should be the bait," Trey says.

"Well, that's stupid, he's not going to kill you, is he?" Cassian says. "I'm the logical option. If he kills me, your Binding's fixed. I'm the one he wants. I'm the textbook bait, so I'll go. Besides, I can shift and hold my own in a fight."

"Fine. You're the courtyard bait," Kato says, walking to join him by the window. "But don't underestimate what a pack of wolves can do. You might be able to fight in a cage, but these guys are trained to fight *as* wolves or whatever their essence is."

In this scene, Eden, the protagonist, while involved in the discussions is not leading them. She's taken a back seat to allow the other characters to make decisions and solidify the plan. It's hard to read; it's almost a surprise when you read "I" as Eden starts talking. It makes the scene jumbled and all over the place. Let's go through it and look at what paragraphs need to change to ensure Eden is getting both the page time she needs and taking the lead as protagonist.

Kato slices Bo's palm, and smears the blood over the dagger, Cassian stands up, walks to the window, and gazes at the courtyard below.

This is a key action, taking blood from Bo is the missing piece the gaggle need in the "final battle"—this should be an action the protagonist takes, not a side character.

The next few paragraphs are fine, it's general discussion and information sharing. The next paragraph where there's an issue is this one:

"Maybe," I say, hoping Arden and Hermia got my messages.
"But he's right—we do need a plan," Trey says.

The reason this is a problem, is because Trey is taking

charge. It's not his job as "love interest" to lead the group towards finalizing a battle plan, that should be the protagonist's job. Sure, no one died and made her leader... EXCEPT I DID AS AUTHOR. That's the point of a protagonist, dammit. They take charge, they drive the group forward—it's their story, they need to reign victorious. Sure, the group works together, but it's the protagonist out front, always. Eden should say Trey's line. We'll correct that shortly. Let's keep going.

The next problematic line is this little puppy:

"So, we need bait. I guess that's Eden," Kato says.

No. For the love of all things literary, absolutely no. The protagonist should be volunteering themselves as sacrificial lamb. Not another character. Why? Because (a) the protagonist should always have to make the biggest sacrifice, (b) choosing to be a sacrifice is a powerful act and if it's foisted upon you, it makes both characters—the foister and the foistee—look weak.

The next line that redirects the scene power is this one:

"No. We need Eden to use the knife on Victor. If one of the wolves gets her before she gets to Victor we're all screwed. I should be the bait," Trey says.

While there's nothing technically wrong with this line, it redirects the power away from Eden. In the previous line, Kato offered Eden as bait. Which means, Trey really ought to be talking directly to Eden—she, after all, is the sacrificial lamb. But instead, he's talking to the group. This lessens her authority as leader and decision maker and essentially detracts from making her the protagonist. Let's look at the final problematic lines:

"Fine. You're the courtyard bait," Kato says, walking to join him by the window. "But don't underestimate what a pack of wolves can do. You might be able to fight in a cage, but these guys are trained to fight *as* wolves or whatever their essence is."

There are a few issues with this. First up, once again Eden is describing the physical movement of another character. She's more or less stayed motionless in this scene, while other characters have had all the movement beats. While of course other characters will move during scenes, it's just another way in which she's cowering in the corner, and observing rather than engaging. We've lessened her scene power by doing this.

Second, Kato is making the decision. He's signing off on Cassian being the bait, thus signing off on the plan. Only the leader, aka your local friendly protagonist, should sign off on the plan and decide who gets to be bait. Once again, her role as protagonist in this scene has been reduced by a side character taking charge. An easy fix to be sure, but another example of how side characters can steal the limelight.

Okay, let's look at the published scene where she is the protagonist and where she holds the scene power:

As I slice Bo's palm and smear the blood over the dagger, Cassian stands up, walks to the window, and gazes at the courtyard below.

"We don't have a plan," he says, "you need a plan before a fight."

"Is that cage fighting wisdom?" Kato growls.

Cassian glances at him; if he notices the irritation in his voice, he doesn't seem bothered by it.

"It's logic," he says, turning to me. "You were lucky Maddison and Arden were there when he attacked last time. This time we're on our own."

"Maybe," I say, hoping Arden and Hermia got my messages. "But you're right—we do need a plan."

Kato finishes bandaging Bo's hand then slumps into the seat next to her and strokes her head.

"Well, Victor was wounded by Arden. So, he won't come on his own, which means he'll bring wolves, and wolves always hunt in packs," I say.

"And they always isolate their prey," Trey adds.

"Right," I nod. "So, we need bait. I guess that's me."

"No. We need you to use the knife on Victor. If one of the wolves gets you before you get to Victor we're all screwed," Trey says. "I should be the bait."

"Well, that's stupid, he's not going to kill you, is he?" Cassian says. "I'm the logical option. If he kills me, your Binding's fixed. I'm the one he wants. I'm the textbook bait, so I'll go. Besides, I can shift and hold my own in a fight."

"Fine. You're the courtyard bait," I say, walking to join him by the window. "But don't underestimate what a pack of wolves can do, Cassian. You might be able to fight in a cage, but these guys are trained to fight *as* wolves or whatever their essence is."

The scene corrects all of the aforementioned issues. Eden is leading the action and taking the much-needed blood from Bo; she's making the decision about who should be bait as well as initially offering herself up as bait. It's a much stronger scene and every character is in their rightful place and it's clear that she is wielding the scene power.

Now, there are some instances where the scene power may not be in the protagonist's hands—these include scenes where the protagonist loses, such as in early interactions with the villain or antagonistic force. In these scenes, the power dynamic can shift in order to reduce the hero or make them feel unworthy, and that's absolutely appropriate at that point in a character arc. They've not defeated their flaw or wound in order to become the hero they need to be. That said, these losses of power should be fleeting and confined to the short interactions with the villain. Outside of these times, the protagonist should always be in charge and driving the plot forward.

Essentially, as long as your side characters don't start taking up the "leader" mantel, you're all good.

But... But... But...

Let's talk about that for a second. Because sometimes, a writer will find that a side character makes waves. Throws tantrums and stomps and rages until we lowly authors pay heed. They demand our attention and scream that they want more, need more. What happens then? How do we combat that and wrangle the tempestuous little fuckers back into line? What if we can't?

You have a few options here. Either you've made a mistake and the character you thought was the main character, is not. It happens; in fact, it happened to me with my first story. I realized it would be better told from another character's perspective. The second I swapped POV, the new protagonist came alive and so did the story.

Or, if that doesn't take your fancy, you can always silence them by telling them you'll give them their own book and story or series at a later date. Or you could strip them back, push them into the background and force them back down again. There's no right or wrong answer, it will depend entirely on your story and series needs.

What I hope is clear from this section is that while your side characters can be on the page and in the scenes as much as the protagonist, what's important is the locus of power and where that sits. It must *always* sit with the protagonist.

3.10 BFFS OR BARELY BUDDIES?

There are many character journeys, but two are more common than most. It's these two I'm going to focus on in relation to side characters: the hero's and the heroine's journeys. Now, these concepts are heavily seated in plot and this book is not a book on plot. If you want to learn more about the journeys and how they affect story structure, then head to the resources section for book recommendations on those topics specifically. The aspect that affects side characters, though, is how the hero versus heroine views relationships. Point to note here, I'm using gendered pronouns but heroes and heroines can be any gender. For example, a famous male character (Harry Potter) goes on a heroine's journey.

What are these supposed journeys?

Well, the heroine's journey is about finding identity and self-worth and connection. The hero's journey is about completing a goal. But what's key in this chapter is how those two journeys interact with side characters.

How Does the Hero View Relationships?

The hero in his journey willingly isolates himself, more often than not he ends up "alone" in some form by the end of the story. Think of Jack Reacher, James Bond and Wonder Woman. Sure, there are side characters in those stories and some repeat characters—like M in James Bond—over the series, but the hero fights the good fight alone and takes the glory for doing so. Characters may interact with him along the way but there is some subtle distance between them. The consequence of this is that while side characters are still important to the story, the hero will ultimately end up isolated (voluntarily) away from his buddies in order to get the job done. And the hero is happy with that.

How Does the Heroine View Relationships?

The heroine is a different beast entirely. Relationships are key for her and her success. Her story focuses on family, connection, and friendship. She belongs to a greater whole—that being the network she fosters. Speaking of network, readers of the genre are often after comfort or a sense of belonging. Think about the *Harry Potter* series–it's created the most enormous fanbase of any work of literature in decades; fans know which Hogwarts house they *belong* to, they buy branded attire to demonstrate their *belonging* to that house.

In her story, the heroine spends her time building, growing, and nurturing her network so that *together* they can defeat the big bad. When isolated, the heroine's story slows and falters—look at the latter books in the *Harry Potter* series, isolated away from his friends, the books grind slower and slower and consequently get longer and longer. But by the end, Harry has brought all his friends and family back together to defeat Voldemort.

The key word being "together." Harry doesn't go to the final show down between him and Voldemort alone, he's with the entire Weasley family, and half the school and all the professors. For a heroine, their community is their everything. She's connected and the power of her connection is what fuels her ability to defeat the villain. It's in the requests for help, the reliance on others, the exchanges of information and support that together forms an unbreakable network. And at the end of the story, the heroine is still with her community. This is what defeats the villain.

Other than Harry Potter, examples of the heroine's journey include: Disney/Pixar movies *Moana*; *Cars*; *Toy Story*; *Monsters, Inc.*; *Onward*; *The Hunger Games* by Suzanne Collins; *Twilight* by Stephanie Meyer; *The Avengers*; the recent Netflix show *Fate: The Winx Saga*; *The Long Way to a Small Angry Planet* by Becky Chambers; *Ocean's Eleven*—in fact many heist stories, most Young Adult literature, and many romance books.

The Role of Side Characters in the Hero's and Heroine's Journey

Key things to note, then, are that side characters play *far* more of a pivotal role in a heroine's journey than a hero's. Ultimately a hero will go it alone at the climax of your story, whereas in the heroine's journey, the side characters will be with her to the end, this means they will play a key role in actually defeating the villain. Heroine stories will have a deeper reliance on side characters and importantly the relationships she fosters with those side characters, love, family, and connection will all play a role or act as themes.

In a heroine's journey, the side characters are key to her journey and the outcome. Though I will say it should still be the heroine herself that makes the final striking blow on a villain's nut sack. She has to take him down because she's the protagonist, despite the fact she's likely to have had help from her loved ones to get there.

Whereas in a hero's journey, side characters are important but less connected to the journey itself. Think of the journeys like dances. In a heroine's journey, it's a waltz, the side characters are connected to and joined to the heroine the entire way through the dance-journey. But in a hero's story, it's more likely to be street dance, the dance crew might bounce off each other, give each other a hand as they flip flop through the moves, but ultimately each dancer dances alone in the crew.

50 Shades of Connection

Regardless of whether you're writing a hero or heroine's journey, it's important to spend at least a little time on your character relationships. How do they connect with each other and are those connections all the same or do they look different?

One tool you have in your character bucket is to consider how your protagonist relates to each individual side character.

The vast majority of writers don't consider this, they keep the protagonist relating to each side character in the same way. But think about it. That's not what happens in real life. Whether you like to admit it or not, it's human nature to moderate yourself depending on the situation you're in and the people you're around. Chances are, you're most relaxed with family and friends (though unfortunately, this isn't always the case). But even with family, you're unlikely to act the same around your parents as you are around your very conservative granny or your hipster aunt. And what about your friendship groups?

I know your type; I've seen you devious rebels before. When you're with your friends, you're more likely to throw a tequila shot back, whip your bra off and jiggle those bajungas while cavorting on the table in Louboutin heels.

Just me?

Awkward.

However, half-naked, drunken table-top dancing isn't acceptable during your family Sunday roast now, is it?

You moderate, I moderate, we all moderate.

Everyone has an office telephone voice for dealing with snotty clients, it's not the same voice we use with our martial arts club and that isn't the same voice for the girls having a gin on a Friday night. Most people have different groups of friends, and different interactions with each of those groups. That's why it's always a little awkward at a wedding until your pole dancing crew have necked a few vino-splashos and lubricated up, it's only then they interact with your conservative club friends.

Examples in Practice

James Bond (a hero) interacts differently with all of his side characters. With M there's a frustrated yet respectful connection, with Q it's usually a take relationship. Q gives James new spy-gadgets and then pleads with him not to smash them up. All the while, James is tampering down Q's geek speak and gathering as many gadgets as possible which he will inevitably smash up later. Then of course you have the bond girls, and well, we all know what those relationships are like *wink, wink, nudge, nudge, licky lips... and yes, this time I meant *those* lips. While none of these characters are with Bond when he's fighting the bad guys, they all play a role in helping him get to the end. M with guidance, Q with gadgets and Bond girls? Well, perhaps they're strengthening his stamina...for erm... later fights?

Moving on. Harry Potter, (as a heroine) has a BFF-style, best friend bromance relationship with Ron, a mutual respect and trusting relationship with Hermione, a "father" from a distance type mentor relationship with Dumbledore, a brother-in-arms type friendship with Neville, and a strained and tense relationship with his relatives Petunia, Vernon, and Dudley. While his family are constant blockers and barriers to him fulfilling his goal, the rest of the gang are all there fighting the good fight with him. Ron and Hermione literally go with him on the quests, and in the first book they both sacrifice themselves to help him reach that final showdown.

Differences Create Characterization and Conflict

The reason for discussing these differences is that you can utilize them to great effect with your rabble of side characters.

Having your protagonist relate to other side characters in a variety of ways enables you to show all the aspects of your protagonist's personality, thus deepen your protagonist's character. Second, it creates varying emotional and tension levels. Third, if your character has multiple relationships and some of them appear deeper, stronger, or better than others, that leads to opportunities for creating conflict through jealousy or resentment.

Each character in your protagonist's inner circle should have a different kind of bond to the protagonist and the other characters.

If your character feels most comfortable with friend A then they're more likely to be open and discuss their feelings. But perhaps they don't feel as secure with friend B. Instead, their friendship is about banter and jokes, and perhaps with friend C, the protagonist is in awe of them and thus spends most of their time trying to impress them. These three relationships would produce very different connections, levels of tension, interactions, and dialogue.

When creating bonds and relationships, consider:

- In jokes between friends
- A baseline emotion or feeling to describe the

relationship: safety, security, humor, lust, trust, respect. Each of these forms a very different type of connection
- Relationship quirks—for example certain words or phrases only those two characters use. Like handshakes, a particular style of messaging, a location that's special, always kissing each other goodbye three times etc.
- Nicknames
- Relationship specific greetings
- Activities the characters only do together
- Secrets only shared between them (this is particularly useful for creating conflict and tension between the secret holders and other characters)
- An adjusted tone of voice or speaking style reserved for just that couple
- A value the two friends share

STEP 3 FLESH AND BLOOD SUMMARY

- Where we Frankensteined our characters, had testicles for ears and nipples for eyes, spat story seeds, played with equations, experienced flashbacks, and foisted foibles on ourselves.
- E + R = O. Event plus reaction equals outcome. This means your side characters need reactions and emotions to the events in your story.
- Pick one or two salient features for your character description and make them stand out and have meaning to the story.
- Relevancy is king—never show the reader something unless it's important; this goes for all the information you describe about your side characters too.
- While your side characters are created to aid your protagonist's story and arc, they need to feel real and whole to the reader too. They need a why—a reason for existing that isn't just to help the protagonist.
- They also need a reason for being in every scene. In other words, they have three levels of why:

- Why are they helping the protagonist?
- What is their life goal / purpose external to the protagonist why?
- Why are they in the scene why?
- Having perfect characters is a cardinal sin, make sure your side characters have flaws, it makes them more relatable. But to make the unlikable appealing, ensure they have at least one positive trait, a relatable wound, a moral line they won't cross, an expertise in something, they demonstrate duty or kindness towards others and have the capacity to change—even if they don't actually change, having the capacity is more important than changing.
- Your major side characters are likely to need origin stories—it shows why they need to change and often explains the reason why they are the way they are and it can create consequences too.

There are some common mistakes with origin stories:

1. Giving too much space to a side character origin story
2. Making the origin story about the character's past instead of the present in the current story
3. Opening your book with the origin story or dropping it too early on

If you're unsure how to create an origin story, here are some questions you can base your thinking on:

- What were the most significant events in your characters past?
- Are there any painful or overly happy memories?
- Who or what influenced the character?

- What kind of home or background does your character come from?
- If you had to pick one emotion to summarize the character's childhood, what would it be?

- There are a number of reasons for and against using flashbacks. See the body of the chapter for them. You can create a trigger to help you get into a flashback and back out of it again.

For side characters, you can:

- Use short flashbacks—and triggers to initiate the flash, like "old" banter or seeing a photograph or an item that jogs a memory.
- Have the protagonist reference a short memory about the side character (make sure it's relevant to the plot though).
- Reference a memory through dialogue.

- When introducing new side characters, make sure you introduce them a number of times, each time focusing on a different aspect of their salient features. Don't just repeat their blue eyes were bright.
- Pick out the unusual aspects of the character that are memorable and focus on describing those.
- Don't be afraid of using humor, there are a ton of different types of humor out there and it brings a new flavor to your story.
- Use items, locations, and emotions to help anchor your side characters in your reader's mind.
- Scene power refers to whoever commands the power in a room—or "scene" in your book. Your

protagonist should always be driving every scene. When you allow side characters to take control of the scene power and drive the plot forward it reads peculiarly, it's messy, and the lines blur. The scene loses its strength because that power is parceled out between characters instead of being concentrated in the protagonist.

- Heroes and heroines view relationships differently. A hero will always isolate himself and therefore relationships are less important to him. The opposite is true of a heroine. For her, relationships are everything; she collects them, nurtures them, and they help see her through to the end of her story. The side characters in a heroine's journey are essential to her completing her arc.
- Remember to vary your character relationships— not all characters should relate to each other in the same way.

Questions to Think About

1. Thinking about your genre, what characters stand out most to you and why?
2. Brainstorm a list of as many side character origin stories as you can. Are there any patterns? Are some things more memorable than others? If so, why?

STEP 4 VOICE OF AN ANGEL

4.0 VOICE OF AN ANGEL

Where we dress in suitably dark latex, carry whips, get stabby over voices, play on train tracks, and have a good ol' gossip.

Spoiler warnings for books: *Six of Crows* by Leigh Bardugo, *A Man Called Ove* by Fredrik Backman, *Harry Potter* series by J.K. Rowling.

Spoiler warnings for TV shows: *The Queen's Gambit*

Voice has always been put on a pedestal like it's a curly haired Goldilocks princess. For many writers, voice is one of the more nuanced and mysterious aspects of craft. It's the intangible skill we all have wet dreams over perfecting. Oh, to be one of those writers people talk about as having such a unique and memorable voice. I don't know about you, but I'd happily get stabby over it.

But voice as a concept is often confused. See, there's "author voice" and then there's "character voice," and there's a 1000-mile-wide chasm of difference between the two. Voice isn't difficult or complex, it doesn't have to be pretentious or smoked by tweed-wearing cigar fans. It's just voice. The problem is that when "voice" or "author voice" is flung around, what most writers really mean is actually "character voice." Let's look at the two.

What Is Author Voice?

An author voice can change, in the most basic of terms, it literally means an author's "style." Let's be real, some days we wake up fabulous, and adorn ourselves in glittery pink G-strings and feather boas and the next we shroud our shame in disproportionately bin-bag-shaped items seven sizes too big.

Author voice is the same. In these craft books, I'm sweary and flighty and prone to bouts of tangential swearing, but in my fiction, I focus more on hope and characters who are teens and diva-like, though I try to keep the banter across all my work. Author voice can flex depending on the genre the author is writing in, or the tone they want to achieve, or the pace at which they want the story to be told.

Look at Nora Roberts or Stephen King—both have written books under pen names and in different genres to their most famous of works. This is because they've written in a different style, for different audiences, meaning the "sound" or their voice is different from one book to the next.

This means that author voice is changeable, it ebbs and flows with the fancies of said author. If an author changes genre, their voice should change too. Children can't read stories written in the voice of an erotica author, can they now? Obviously, it will change.

An author's voice is simply the culmination of all aspects of their craft and prose choices. For example, the sound of their voice will include things like:

- Their choice of verbs and adjectives
- The pattern of their punctuation and grammar (one author might choose to use Oxford commas, another might refuse)
- Use or not of adverbs
- Length of sentences
- The balance of dialogue to prose
- Accented dialogue or not
- The quantity of descriptive prose
- The style of their prose. Is it full of metaphors or do they use a cleaner style of description?
- The size of their cast of characters
- POV

What Is Character Voice?

Character voice is not changeable. A character's voice is *who* they are. If they're a nerdy astrophysicist who always uses ridiculously big words, they're still going to be an astrophysicist who uses ridiculously big words at the end of the story no matter how they've grown or changed as a person in the story. All a character has is their voice on the page to define and describe who they are. When you change that, you fundamentally change who that character is. They no longer sound like them. If our nerdy astrophysicist dropped the big words and started using gang slang, it would read like another character entirely.

But here is the problem for side characters. Protagonists get three to four hundred pages to define and explore their voice. They have pages and pages to refine and portray who they are and their change. Side characters, however, do not. Which means their voices need to be sharp, chiseled, and refined from the get go. We need them to know who they are so the protagonist can explore who she is during the story.

Too often, what happens is a writer will focus on creating the ideal hero for their story. They spend time cultivating a unique voice for the protagonist and then slap on a few side characters on the side to make the hero look good. Problem with that is if you took away the dialogue tags or the narrative identifiers all your side characters would be indistinguishable. In fact, J. Thorn and Jeff Elkins, fellow indie authors, coined the term "monomouth" to describe this phenomenon of characters all sounding the same. They were predominantly talking about dialogue. But the word serves the same purpose here. Side character voice is rarely given more than a passing thought, let alone sculpted into a precision literary tool.

Let's look at an example. Hermione Granger, a major side character from *Harry Potter,* sounds clever. She's always sharing tidbits of spells and knowledge. She also sounds bossy, patronizing, and like a know-it-all—all accurate representations of her personality. But compare her to Dr. Watson from *Sherlock Holmes,* and while both are clever characters, Watson is far more patient and sensitive than Hermione.

That's what we're going to examine here. We're going to focus on honing major side character voices. We'll make them distinct, unique, and defined enough they could chisel the frozen nipples off an abominable snowman.

Character Voice Exercise

One exercise I particularly like is to allow the character to tell you their backstory in their voice. Imagine they're talking to you, telling you their origin story or how they came to be in the location your story is set, or perhaps ask them about an emotional event from their past, that's usually when we see into the soul of a person most.

How would *they* tell you the story? Do they flounder and talk in circles? Are they cheap with their words and use little description or detail? Do they have an accent? Or use particular phrases?

Allowing a character to tell you their backstory in their own voice not only helps you shape the character's voice, it also helps you create their backstory.

Here's an example, from my own work. This is Pearl Rafferty, a side character from *The Scent of Death*. I'm going to run this exercise to hear from her, I've no idea where this is going to go. Maybe it won't reveal anything, maybe it will and I'll chuck it in the book. The purpose, though, is to see how the exercise works in practice. *Note it's written in British English.*

SACHA: Hey, Pearl, can you tell me a little bit about your family life?

PEARL: Most people think I'm some super stuck-up rich girl, because I've got a few designer knickknacks and that. You probably think that too. But I swear I ain't. The only reason we even have the house we have is because some old Scottish relative—none of us had any idea existed—copped it and dad was her only living relative. So down came a wad of cash and a random property she owned in London. Turned out aforementioned random property was a rather lush town house in Hampstead which is probably worth more than the GDP of that obscure country off the arse end of whatever it's called.

Point is, we were just lucky. But that's why both my parents always taught me that random acts of kindness shouldn't be random at all, but intentional and frequent. Dad's a [????]. As for Mum, well she always wanted another kid and couldn't have one, what with her dodgy ovaries, so she trained as a child minder at first, and now she's trying to foster kids and that.

We're one of them families that look like we got

everything, but I still remember tough times as a kid. Mum never earned much money, and dad isn't exactly rolling in it, he fucks about with plants all day. Mum had to get my school clothes from charities when I was a kid. And while a lovely house in Hampstead is obvs in a nice area, the upkeep is well expensive. Don't get me wrong, I've had it good growing up, not like Mal. I've always had warm arms and clean clothes that fit me. God, it kills me that Mal's trousers don't fit him again and his fucking mum spends money on alcohol instead of clothes for him. Not that I could ever say that to him, of course. Yeah, that's what I'll do. I'll ask mum to buy him a new pair and post them to him and just not tell him it was us.

Anyway, my point was, I might look wealthy on the outside, but I'm nothing like that stuck-up rich twat Tina Myers.

I could let Pearl keep going, it's amazing what happens when you let a character just go for it. They reveal loads. And yet, I spend much of my time reluctant to just write exploratively, but when I do, I always learn something about my characters, which inevitably makes it into the book. I guess like real humans, if we're honest, we all like talking about ourselves. I'll have to continue to let her get out everything she wants to say later. For now, although that is a completely raw first draft —yes, I'm sharing a first draft of something—I wanted you to see how the exploratory exercise works in practice. Yes, I've left question marks in there because I didn't know what her dad's job was at the time and it wasn't important enough to stop the flow of words. I know more about her now, and more about her family life than before. I can hear her London twang, even though it needs work. And last, there are threads in that excerpt I could pull into the main story or use to develop her characterization.

Let us slide into the gooey intestinal sludge of side character voice and examine how we can develop and create slick, sexy, sultry, supercharged side character voices.

4.1 THE SIDE CHARACTER LENS

In *10 Steps to Hero*, I pulled out my town crier's outfit and declared true a concept called "the hero lens." While in that book it was in reference to building a protagonist, there's a handy thing or two we can take from it into the creation of side characters. But Sacha, what's a hero lens? I'm delighted you asked...

The Hero Lens

"Everything the hero does, sees, feels and thinks, encloses your reader into a tiny literary lens. Nothing happens in your book unless your protagonist experiences it. Everything is channeled through her. She is the lens your reader looks through when reading your story. Readers want this lens. They covet it." Sacha Black, *10 Steps to Hero: How to Craft Kickass Protagonists*

The hero lens is made up of four parts:

1. Actions

This includes any actions, physical movement, or body language your character does.

2. Thoughts

This includes both inner monologues usually denoted by the use of italics, as well as POV character narration.

3. Dialogue

Does what it says on the tin, anything spoken out loud.

4. Feelings

This includes any emotional showing, telling, visceral reactions, and sensations.

These four are wholly unique to each character and your character's personality should be reflected through them and that's regardless of whether they are the protagonist, a character who isn't a protagonist but still narrates in their own POV, or a standard side character who doesn't narrate through a POV.

Clears throat

Loosens vocal cords with whiskey

Any character who narrates part of the story has a lens.

That's important. "Lenses" are not reserved just for protagonists. And in fact, even characters who *don't* narrate have a lens, it's just not a narrational one.

To save any confusion, we'll keep the protagonist and narrators lenses as the *hero lens* and any other character who doesn't narrate as a *character lens*.

The Character Lens

The character lens is the papery sheaf your side character voices burst through in a fit of mythological god-like savagery. While a character lens still has the same four elements as a hero lens, they're split over two levels. This is because non-POV characters do not have the capacity to let a reader inside their head as a hero. The levels are thus:

Level 1: action and dialogue
Level 2: feelings and thoughts

We'll cover these more specifically and in detail in the next section. For now, what does the lens look like in practice? Let's take two different characters, a protagonist and a side character without a POV. Train tracks are dangerous, mama always told me not to play on them, so let's slap our characters there *cackles*. We'll make it even more dangerous by plopping the devils somewhere remote, like in the middle of the woods. Play ball wordsmiths:

Protagonist:

The track swept through the middle of the forest in an endless curve toward the horizon. Rows and rows of wooden teeth jutted out from under the tracks like six-year-old nightmares. Wind howled like wolves through the trees, I pulled my jacket tighter, gripping my phone deep in my pocket, praying I still had signal.

Let's go through line by line and explore how this demonstrates each element of the character lens.

The track swept through the middle of the forest in an endless curve toward the horizon. [*this is scene setting and the only hint of personality comes from the word endless which indicates some emotional hesitation towards the track and the forest—let's call it subtext shall we!]* Rows and rows of wooden teeth jutted out from under the tracks like six-year-old nightmares. *[This is the first indication of characterization; rather than describing the wood or the color or perhaps the shape as something harmless, the character is describing the tracks like a nightmare. This augments that first hint of subtext in the previous sentence. This also shows the reader that the character is probably a bit of a wimp and feeling scared rather than being brave or nonplussed].* Wind howled like wolves through the trees, *[sensory description and also another reference to a "monster" showing the character's narrative thoughts are about monsters rather than admiring the scenery].* I pulled my jacket tighter, gripping my phone deep in my pocket, *[this action shows the character's feeling scared and reaching for security/comfort].* praying I still had signal. *[Another action indicative of the character's state of mind].*

We don't see dialogue but we will in the next snippet that follows on from the above scene.

Including a Non-POV Side Character

Jackson bounced out of the woods and onto the track. His eyes glittered as he slipped onto the sleepers.
"Get off the track, Jackson, what if a train comes?" I said.
"Chill out. This is amazing." Jumping between the two metallic tracks, his face was bright and wide even in the dimming light.

Once again, let's go through this paragraph and demonstrate how we're using the character and hero lenses to create characterizations and show character.

Jackson bounced out of the woods [*this is the protagonist narrating but Jackson's action of bouncing shows a stark contrast to the narrator's fearful movements*] and onto the track. His eyes glittering as he slipped onto the sleepers. [*Again, while narrated by the protagonist, his actions and body language show that he is feeling excited and not fearful in any way. Specifically, glittering eyes suggest mischief as opposed to fear*].

"Get off the track, Jackson, what if a train comes?" I said. [*It's the first bit of dialogue from the protagonist, but it instantly mimics the feelings we've seen in the previous paragraph, ever fearful, this time for Jackson*].

"Chill out. This is amazing," [*a clear difference in tone and word choice, his dialogue reflects how he feels. "Chill out" indicates that Jackson thinks the protagonist is over reacting*]. Jumping between the two metallic tracks, his face was bright and wide even in the dimming light. [*This final line shows both how Jackson is feeling through his body language and the protagonist's fear of their current situation. The "dimming light" is subtext and foreshadowing for all the monsters that come out at night. The protagonist's narration serves doubly here as a character reveal for both of them*].

In the above section, Jackson displays action and dialogue. It's through those body language actions and his dialogue that we infer the level two aspects of his character lens. We infer that he's feeling excited and thinking about what fun he can get up to even though he himself hasn't told us and we're not seeing that through his point of view.

Let's shimmy into a bit more detail about the character lens.

4.2 CHARACTER LENS AS A NON-POV SIDE CHARACTER

Side characters who don't narrate aspects of the story are little literary taskmasters. Imagine them, if you will, dressed in suitably dark latex, carrying a whip or two and flailing you every time you beg them to show their voice.

These fellas have less page time and less direct contact with the reader than POV characters and protagonists. As the author, you don't have direct access to their character lens; your hands are behind your back, you're restricted, handcuffed, tied up... let's move on before it gets kinky...

Character Lens as a Non-POV Character

Just because you don't have a full "hero" lens for non-point of view characters, doesn't mean you slack off and put no effort into creating their voice. By Jove son, you can still weave a masterful voice for your non-POV character.

If you don't have the character lens, what do you have?

Well, you still have *some* elements of the lens. I mention in the last section that a character lens is broken down like this:

Level 1: action and dialogue
Level 2: feelings and thoughts

I've split the character lens levels by immediacy and control. Level 1—the side character controls themselves and these tactics create immediacy for the reader. Level 2—is displayed far more through narration and interpretation and is therefore less immediate for the reader.

And lest we get amnesic, we have a character's physical appearance which helps to increase their characterization. You can use subtext, their quirks and habits—although these are described by whoever is narrating.

Level 1—Action and Dialogue

Even though we experience a story through a POV character lens, there are two aspects of a lens that any character can control for themselves. No matter who is narrating, side characters are in charge of displaying their own actions and dialogue; they are also story elements that increase immediacy with the reader. This means action and dialogue are your primary tools for crafting a non-POV character's voice and personality.

I'm not going to cover dialogue here; I've reserved that for section 4.3. Let's take a moment to look at action.

Creating Action Through Emotion and Personality

There's that trite saying "actions speak louder than words" and it's true for your characters too. I hate these old sayings, they're like stuffy professors with excessive beards smothered in cake crumbs and a stale odor emanating from them. They might be right but they're also annoying. While "actions speak louder than words" is a cliché, we'll work around it because it's a solid truism if ever I heard one. One of the best ways to show your side character's personality and voice is through their actions.

Action is usually created through two core aspects: personality traits and emotion. To create realistic actions that help deepen characterization you need to *show* their personality rather than telling it. For example, telling it would look a bit like this:

> "Sally was that sort of person; she always took unnecessary risks."

This tells the reader about Sally. But that's so dull. You're not Hitler, or Ghengis Khan, or Kim Jong-il—it's not engaging for the reader to be dictated to. Why not show Sally's behavior through her actions. Maybe on a night out she decides to sneak into an exclusive club through the back, dragging her friends and the protagonist with her. Maybe Sally spots the club owner, and decides they should chat him up, maybe she decides to get blind drunk and take drugs. To up the ante, let her actions impact the protagonist. Perhaps the protagonist has an important audition the next day and is desperate to go home but doesn't want to abandon her friend. Perhaps Sally gets into a fight and the protagonist jumps in to save her, only to get punched and develop a black eye ready for their audition the next day.

A great example of showing personality through action comes from Jolene, an orphan and side character in the recent *The Queen's Gambit* show on Netflix. Jolene spends much of her time enabling the protagonist—Beth, who is also an orphan—via risk taking. Later in the series, Jolene takes a risk by giving Beth a lump sum of money to go to the Soviet Union and play in a big chess competition. Jolene gives Beth the money despite the fact Beth has been displaying a plethora of unreliable behaviors: drinking, drug taking, generally being a mess. But

Jolene believes in Beth so she loans her the money. If Beth wins, she'll give the money back, if she doesn't then Jolene loses her cash. Rather than just having Beth state in dialogue that Jolene is an enabler and takes risks, the film-makers show the viewer through her actions. Jolene enables Beth earlier in the series by smuggling—now illegal—tranquilizers to help her stay calm during some of the chess competitions.

If you're unsure what action a side character's personality traits might take, then another trick you can use is to ask yourself what emotion that character would feel in that moment. What would an angry person do? Would they ball their fists? Sprinkle chili in his mistress's eye cream? Maybe they'd kick an orphan in the nuts or poke their finger in your mouth mid-yawn. What would a jealous person do? Would they throw squirrel blood on a girl's dress? Would they try to sabotage someone's work? If they're sad, would they shout and throw things or cry and retreat into isolation?

Emotions drive actions. If you're ever stuck with how to display a side character's actions ask yourself:

- What is my character feeling in this moment?
- What is the expected emotional reaction?
- How can I subvert that expectation?
- Can I identify five different actions my character would take based on their current emotion?

Level 2—Feelings and Thoughts

Unfortunately, you can only experience accurate feelings and thoughts when you're in the mind and POV of that character with two exceptions:

- Omniscient POV when your narrator is god-like and knows all, sees all and can tell the reader all about

every character's feelings. Which means while the reader—and protagonist—can see how a non-POV character *might* be feeling or what they *might* be thinking, it is just that—"a might."
- Your side character states how they're feeling or what they're thinking in dialogue.

The reader is at the whim of whoever is narrating. Observations of another character's feelings and thoughts are subject to interpretation—the narrators. This is both a good and bad thing. First up, your protagonist will be able to sprinkle interpretation glitter on the story—and, thus, misinterpret—your side characters thoughts and feelings. This means you'll be able to create tension and conflict using the misinterpretations. Furthermore, you can tell a lot about a character—namely your protagonist here—by the way they interpret another character's behavior. Is your protagonist defensive? Have they been too sensitive in how they've interpreted something? Awesome. This will show the reader both that the protagonist is sensitive and that the side character isn't the asshole your protagonist thinks she is.

Subtext

Subtext is vitally important for showing aspects of character and story that you don't want to slap your reader around the face with. We've discussed subtext before, so I won't go into too much detail here; suffice to say, you can use subtext to let the reader infer what a non-POV character might be thinking or feeling through descriptions of body language, what's not said, choreography, and narrating character's interpretations.

One of the best ways to create subtext is by showing your reader what your character is focused on. And that goes for both your narrating character and the side character being described. If, say, your side character is more focused on the exits in a room than the decoration on the wall or the conversation at hand, then the subtext is that the character wants to leave and yet you haven't actually said that in the narration.

Habits and Quirks

Another tool in your box for deepening characterization for a non-POV side character is to ensure they have habits and quirks.

"A habit is a routine movement, action or behavior often done in a repeated pattern. It's automatic and something a reader would deem normal. For example, pushing your glasses up, checking the doors are locked before bed or always reading the newspaper in the morning." Sacha Black, *10 Steps to Hero: How to Craft a Kickass Protagonist.*

"A quirk is unique and idiosyncratic to your character; it's a deliberate behavior. Usually, it will stick out to your reader or other characters. For example, in the movie *East is East*, one character, a young boy called Sajid, refuses to take his jacket off, EVER. He wears it rain, snow, sun or sleeping." Sacha Black, *10 Steps to Hero: How to Craft a Kickass Protagonist.*

Habits are cute, but quirks are *far* cuter—they're better at creating characterization quickly and deeply. Quirks are unusual and thus unexpected, which by their very nature calls attention to them, meaning they're more likely to distinguish one side character from another.

You do have a risk with quirks—if you just throw them out without thought they can fall flat with readers. To combat that, there are two aspects you need to create believable quirks:

- The first is to ensure the quirk has a function in your story

Connect the quirk to your side character's flaw or strength. In section 8.1, I refer to Kaz Brekker from *Six of Crows*. His wound and flaw are represented tangibly through the constant wearing of gloves, which happens to be a quirk too. Monica Geller in *Friends* cleans obsessively, but her cleaning serves a purpose—she usually thinks and works out problems while cleaning.

- The second is to show rather than tell the quirk

As with any "important" element in your book, you need to show rather than tell the reader. For a detailed breakdown of show versus tell, read step 4 in *The Anatomy of Prose*. Just like with action above, you can show the reader how your side character interacts with their quirk, rather than stating it as a fact. Kaz's gloves are referenced by a number of side characters—the reader is shown their importance when he's forced to take them off—and this of course has an emotional consequence.

4.3 GENERAL CHIT CHAT AND
WHAT NOT

I remember the first time I stumbled upon this quote. The world tilted, time slowed to a blurred slush of paradoxical jiggery pokery, and my brain shattered into a thousand tiny writer-pieces.

> "Dialogue is communication between characters, not communication between the writer and reader. Do not confuse the two." Gabriela Pereira, *DIY MFA: Write with Focus, Read with Purpose, Build your Community*.

The quote rocked my world because I'd never considered the fact that dialogue actually had nothing to do with me as the author. Sure, the words are coming from my brain, but they shouldn't sound like me, they shouldn't be *my* words.

Why is this relevant? Well, for one, your side characters—the important ones—need their own unique voices, but also the implication is that your side characters can have their own conversations between each other and about each other.

Your readers can eavesdrop on your characters talking about each other. When they do this, it tells the reader both about the character they're talking about and also about the characters speaking.

If they're sassy bitches and slagging off their friends it tells the reader more about their personality then you ever could by stating they're a bitchy sass queen.

But dialogue is more; it heightens pace, it gives scenes depth and it tells you about characters because it *is* their voice.

Chatting Bollocks

Listen, we all like to chat bollocks, I mean what's better than a glass of vino splasho, a gaggle of your besties and a good gossip about absolute bollocking nonsense? Hell, we all like to indulge in a spot of hyperbole occasionally, why shouldn't your characters?

Because they shouldn't, *Karen*.

NOT. EVER.

In a story every word, sentence, and paragraph should be used to greatest effect. Dialogue needs to be sharp. By its nature, dialogue is pacy, it helps to keep your story running quickly. If you fill it with hot air and gossip girl anecdotes about how your neighbor's cat's girlfriend has fingernails instead of claws, it's going to slow the story down immeasurably.

That means you need to get rid of the redundant. Sack the six-line "hello how are you," nonsense and dive into the good shit. Your readers will thank you. So will your bank balance when your dialogue is tight enough it sells a gazillion books and showers your naked dollar-covered nipples in gin and liquid gold lubricant.

Dialogue exposition—like, "oh Alfred, **I'm sure you know** that Winnie used to steal pantyhose from prostitutes, but..."— should be at a minimum. Yes, sometimes exposition needs to happen. But each and every line you spill onto the page should have a purpose. Is it ratcheting up the tension? Is it conveying information? Spreading lies? Inciting conflict?

Side character Dialogue. Must. Have. A. Purpose—in fact, all dialogue should.

If it doesn't, it creates boring conversations. Wandering dialogue is only fun on Friday nights with friends. Not in books.

It's less effective at deepening characterization too.

Dialogue

I mentioned the term "monomouth" earlier. I rather like the phrase. It means your characters all sound the same. In fact, that's an excellent exercise to start with. I challenge you, oh worthy wordsmith, to pull apart a dialogue-heavy section of your story. Strip out any description, any dialogue tags, and leave just the dialogue on the page. Now tell me, can you tell who is speaking? Perhaps you can, because you know your story intimately. But hand your manuscript to someone else, perhaps a partner, a secretary, a work colleague, a secret lover with a fetish for sultry whispered stories. Now tell me, could they tell the difference?

If they could, congratulations, you get to be a smug prick this evening, safe in the knowledge your characters all sounded delightfully unique.

If, however, you're like the vast majority of the writing population and your characters had a rather virulent case of monomouth, then welcome to the club. I have the same problem in the first book I ever wrote. It happens, we learn.

Dialogue is even more important for side characters because of their lack of page time. We've already established that they need to be them but BIGGER. They need to be all character, all uniqueness all the time in order to stand out.

I asked Jeff Elkins, aka The Dialogue Doctor, what was

important when creating side character dialogue. This is what he said:

"When writing a side character's voice, we should first consider what type of side character they are. Is the side character an ongoing ally in the story or is your side character a one-off character who will only appear in a specific scene?

One-off side characters are fun because they allow us to appreciate something about your protagonist's voice. To do this, we should make the one-off character's voice an extreme opposite in some way to our protagonist. The reader will only have to live with this one-off character for a single scene, going to an extreme with the voice will not make the reader feel distant from the character.

If your protagonist is dark and brooding, make your one-off side character chipper and optimistic. If your protagonist is a go-getting optimist, make your side character a disengaged depressive. Forcing your protagonist into a conversation with his/her/their opposite will accentuate your protagonist's voice and engage the reader in a deeper way. For example, Fredrik Backman's *A Man Called Ove* opens with Backman's grumpy, aging, impatient protagonist and opens the book by tangling with a young, positive, sales clerk. By pairing his protagonist with an opposite one-off side character, as readers, we get an immediate feel for Ove's voice.

Long-lasting side characters are a different ball game. It isn't enough to make their voices different than your protagonist's voice because the reader will need to live with these side characters. We want your reader to empathize with them as much (if not more) than they do with your protagonist. The key to writing long-lasting side characters is strategically creating voices that will complement and contrast with your protagonist's voice, so that your long-lasting side characters will naturally encourage your protagonist and challenge your protagonist toward change and maturity.

In order to complement your protagonist, your long-lasting side characters need to share a common mission or desire with your protagonist. This commonality should show in the side characters' voices. For example, in JK Rowling's Harry Potter, Harry, Hermione and Ron all feel like outcast-underdogs who have something to prove. The three characters become a unit because it is them against the world as they seek their destinies together.

At the same time, if Harry were left to his own devices, he would grow sullen, angry, and isolated. In this way, Ron and Hermione are the perfect side characters to challenge him. Hermione lends her drive and "never surrender" attitude to Harry, while Ron brings a deep appreciation of family and connection to the team. If merged together, the two side characters are what Rowling wants her protagonist to become, making the three characters the perfect hero for the story.

When creating these voices, know who you want your protagonist to mature into, and provide shades of what your protagonist is missing in the voices of their side-character allies. If you do, when you are writing an intense scene, you will find the side-character will naturally seek to spur your protagonist on to victory over the barriers standing in the way." *Jeff Elkins, The Dialogue Doctor.*

If you've not read my book *The Anatomy of Prose*, there is an entire section in it—Step 5—that provides a deep dive for improving your dialogue. Let's look at some tricks you can use to differentiate your side character dialogue.

Background Is Everything

First up, understand your character's background. Their history and past and where they come from is everything when determining how they sound.

Dialect and Accents

Some of you will shudder at the prospect of using an accent, others will revel in it; wherever you sit on that spectrum, a word of caution in using them. They're notoriously hard to keep up for the duration of your novel. Most authors will start with a fine accent and then it slips as it becomes grueling to write. Better to pick a couple of words or a hint at the accent and sprinkle it into the text rather than risk offending native speakers or overkilling the accent and making your book difficult to read.

There is a certain sound to a "posh" British over-enunciated accent littered with unnecessarily pompous words, and it sounds rather different to a Saaaff Laandan accent. American English sounds far more relaxed than British English; Australian and Canadian English sound different again. Non-native English speakers often have heavily accented dialogue and will sprinkle in the occasional non-English word into their speech.

The point is, there are rhythms and patterns to these regional dialects. Study them. Listen to language. This might sound nonsense, but I associate a letter or sound with different dialects. For example, when I hear a cockney speaker in my mind's eye, I connect it with the letter A. Why? Well, look at the phrase above "Saaaff Landaan" (south London) and tell me you didn't hear a cockney voice? Exactly. In my imagination, New York is O and a southern American drawl is the "all" as in y'all sound. A posh British accent is an "orf" sound.

One Christmas Day, a load of fox hunting horse riders trampled through our garden while hunting. My mom went outside, holding a shotgun over her arm (we lived on a farm then) pissed that her winter greens were being smushed by hooves. The lead rider tipped his hat and said "Good Day." Mama Black's irritated and delightfully posh British response was "Fark Orff." As the rider's face dropped, I fell about cackling and it was at that moment the "orrf" sound was solidified.

You don't have to create a sound association for an accent, but it helps me evoke the sound I want in dialogue. If you know a posh British accent is enunciated to its pinnacle in that "orf" sound then picking and choosing phrases that help recreate that sound will help you sprinkle in a lashing of accented sound without fannying around with spelling changes.

Personality at the Sentence Level

Personality can and should be reflected at the sentence level. The easiest way to demonstrate this is with a stark comparison between characters. Collect word bags for your little deviants. Let's say you have an academic type character. How do you create their voice? What would they sound like? Let's call him Professor Stuffy.

Professor Stuffy's word bag would look something like this:

Furthermore, equally, in addition, hasten to add, pertinent, subject to requirements, additionally, moreover.

If I were writing Professor Stuffy, I'd make a note, be it mental or written, about his tone, structural dialogue, and narration like this:

Stuffy uses long sentences in his dialogue, always over explaining, or using complex words when simple ones would do. He uses lots of commas because all his sentences are run on. Other characters often end up cutting him off because he waffles and they explain for him. He sounds dry because of an overuse of long words. Whenever he explains he always counter explains, meaning he'll argue a for and against which is very academic and entirely unhelpful to his colleagues. He'd probably sound a little something like this:

"I refuse to discuss the matter further. Whether or not you prefer to divulge your promiscuous exploits or not, I shan't be subjected to it, it's not appropriate dinner conversation."

But let's say you have a different character, Michaela. Someone who is a woman of few words, blunt, always gets right to the point, and prefers not to be subjected to waffle. She's likely to use short sentences, as few words as possible. It's likely she doesn't need commas because her sentences are too short, so there will be lots of staccato periods and choppy dialogue. She sounds cold and brutal, just like her personality! She'd probably say the same sentence above but something like this:

"No one cares who you fucked."

How do we pull this together? Here are some questions to help you create a tone and voice for your side characters:

- What common words would they use?
- Do they use slang?
- What's their background both locationally and professionally?
- Do they use long sentences (in which case you would punctuate with lots of commas) or choppy short ones (punctuated with lots of periods)?
- How would you describe the tone of their voice?
- What letter do you associate with the sound of their voice?

You choose personality traits for a reason, allow those personality traits to influence the word choices you make at the sentence level. For example, if you have an angry soldier character, they're likely to use a lot of onomatopoeia, violent word choices, or descriptions. Instead of choosing to describe a tree as a flowing watercolor, leaves drifting to the earth like paint drops, they might call it a haggard soldier standing, twisted and tired, at attention. Personality is voice. Allow it to take charge, allow it to influence your characters at every level of your story.

STEP 4 VOICE OF AN ANGEL SUMMARY

- Where we dressed in suitably dark latex, carried whips, got stabby over voices, played on train tracks, and had a good ol' gossip.
- Author voice is changeable. It ebbs and flows with the fancies of the author and the genre they're writing in.

Voice is the culmination of all aspects of craft. Including:

- Verbs and adjectives
- Punctuation and grammar (one author might choose to use Oxford commas, another might refuse)
- Use or not of adverbs
- Length of sentences
- The balance of dialogue to prose
- Accented dialogue or not
- The quantity of descriptive prose
- The style of your prose, is it full of metaphors or do you use a cleaner style of description?

- The size of your cast of characters
- POV

- Character voice is not changeable. Their voice is *who* they are.
- Allow your character to tell you their backstory in their voice. How would *they* tell you the story?

- The hero lens is made up of four parts:

1. Actions
This includes any actions, physical movement, or body language your character does.
2. Thoughts
This includes both inner monologues, usually denoted by the use of italics, as well as POV character narration.
3. Dialogue
Does what it says on the tin, anything spoken out loud.
4. Feelings
This includes any emotional showing, telling, visceral reactions, and sensations.

- While a character lens still has the same four elements as a hero lens, they're split over two levels. This is because non-POV characters do not have the capacity to let a reader inside their head. The levels are thus:

Level 1: action and dialogue
Level 2: feelings and thoughts

- No matter who is narrating, side characters are in charge of displaying their own actions and dialogue; they're also story elements that increase immediacy with the reader. This means action and dialogue are your primary tools for crafting a non-POV character's voice and personality.

- Actions speak louder than words. To create realistic actions that help deepen characterization you need to *show* their personality rather than telling it.

Emotions drive actions. If you're ever stuck with how to display a side character's actions ask yourself:

- What is my character feeling in this moment?
- What is the expected emotional reaction?
- How can I subvert that expectation?
- Can I identify five different actions my character would take based on their current emotion?

You can only experience accurate feelings and thoughts when you're in the mind and POV of that character with two exceptions:

- Omniscient POV when your narrator is god-like and know all, sees all, and can tell the reader all about every character's feelings. Which means while the reader—and protagonist—can see how a non-POV character *might* be feeling or what they *might* be thinking, it is just "a might."
- Your side character states how they're feeling or what they're thinking in dialogue.

- Subtext helps you show aspects of character and story that you don't want to slap your reader around the face with.
- A habit is a routine movement, action, or behavior often done in a repeated pattern.

- A quirk is unique and idiosyncratic to your character; it's a deliberate behavior and much more useful for displaying characterization.

There are two aspects you need to create believable quirks:

- The first is to ensure the quirk has a function in your story
- The second is to show rather than tell the quirk

- Don't let your side characters have conversation that serves no purpose.
- Check your stories for monomouth.
- Make minor character's voices opposite in sound, tone, and style to your protagonist's. This helps both characters shine.

- "The key to writing long-lasting side characters is strategically creating voices that will complement and contrast with your protagonist's voice, so that your long-lasting side characters will naturally encourage your protagonist and challenge your protagonist toward change and maturity." Jeff Elkins, *The Dialogue Doctor*.

- Consider your side character's background when creating their voice and spoken dialogue. How does it impact their word choice, tone, and accent?
- Consider creating a word bag for your side characters.

Here are some questions to help you create a tone and voice for your side characters:

- What common words would they use?
- Do they use slang?
- What's their background both locationally and professionally?
- Do they use long rambling sentences (in which case you would punctuate with lots of commas) or choppy short ones (punctuated with lots of periods)?
- How would you describe the tone of their voice?
- What letter do you associate with the sound of their voice?

Questions to Think About

1. Create a word bag for your most significant side characters
2. Examine one of your favorite books in your genre, what elements of their character help to show their voice?

STEP 5 WHAT DO SIDE CHARACTERS DO ANYWAY?

5.0 WHAT DO SIDE CHARACTERS DO ANYWAY?

In which we brush Barbie's hair, send messages via gods, see the world in a new light, and pepper the hero's path with obstacles.

Spoiler warnings for books: *Lord of the Rings* by J.R.R. Tolkien, *Game of Thrones* by George R.R. Martin, *Of Mice and Men* by John Steinbeck, *The Jungle Book* by Rudyard Kipling, *Siege and Storm* by Leigh Bardugo, *Roseblood* by A.G. Howard, *Dracula* by Bram Stoker, *Illuminae* by Jay Kristoff and Amie Kaufman, *An Unkindness of Magicians* by Kat Howard, *Percy Jackson and the Lightning Thief* by Rick Riordan, *The House in the Cerulean Sea* by T.J. Klune

Spoiler warnings for movies: *Mean Girls, Fatal Attraction, The Usual Suspects, The Lion King, Indiana Jones, Frozen, I Am Legend, Castaway, Fight Club, Black Panther, When Harry Met Sally*

Spoiler warnings for TV show: *Once Upon a Time, Buffy the Vampire Slayer*

What Is an Archetype?

If you've read *10 Steps to Hero: How to Craft a Kickass Protagonist,* then you'll know hero archetypes in their purest sense don't exist. However, archetypes do still exist. **Archetypes are masks worn by characters to serve a particular function at a particular time to move the plot forward.** In other words, they're a literary device. Which happens to be what side characters are and unsurprisingly why you find archetypes in side characters.

I know, shocking isn't it!

The most common mistake writers make with archetypes is assuming that if you pop an archetypal hat on a character that they must stay that way forevermore. Not so, while yes, it does help with character consistency and that helps with characterization and depth, it's not like your virginity—you *can* take an archetype back. That's especially the case in a series. Once you've written a couple of books in a series you still want your characters to grow and develop to keep the reader interested. Allowing them to grow and develop out of one archetype and into another is totally allowed.

> "Think of it [archetypes] as character cosplay for story pace. If you forced a character to act as a mentor to the hero for the entire plot and only that, you're squeezing your character into such a tiny box you flatten them, literally and figuratively. One of the goals of a wordsmith is to create three-dimensional, rounded characters. That means pouring complexity into a character's design. Forcing your hero or another character to serve one purpose only is simplistic at best and, at worst, traitorous to your novel's potential." Sacha Black, *10 Steps to Hero: How to Craft a Kickass Protagonist.*

5.1 THE BEST FRIEND FOREVER / SIDEKICK

It's unusual for a protagonist not to have a best friend, or if not "best friend" specifically, then a character who is close to them. Everyone needs someone to tell them they're being a bint, or hand them a tub of Ben and Jerry's, a life-size poster of their ex and a delightful array of sharp objects to throw at said poster.

Even in *I Am Legend*, where a lone survivor—Will Smith—spends much of the film on his own, he still had a doggie-sized BFF. Likewise in *Castaway*, Tom Hanks who quite literally spent 95% of the film on his own had Wilson, the volleyball head. There's a reason you don't have a single character protagonist in a story.

It's a good point to recognize that, while you can create stories without many characters, they tend to suffer from one major issue—a lack of pace. One of the core reasons for that is, if there isn't anyone around, there ain't no one to talk to. This means less stabbing, less looks of death and less of the really important stuff: conflict. It also means very few opportunities for dialogue, which is a surefire way to up the pace in any scene.

Even when you have lone wolf characters like James Bond

—who doesn't really have a "friend" in the classic sense—ol' Bondy still has rampant sexual shenanigans with Bond Girlios and a slew of connections with other characters around him. If I've said it once, I'll say it again, everyone knows that wolves live in packs and islands are formed in clusters.

It's almost impossible to create a story with a single character. Why? Because people—characters—create the force, pressure, and tension needed to nudge a hero into changing. Without external force, humans don't change. We're lazy fucks, happy to sit in our havens, what we know, like, and enjoy is safe and comfortable. It's boring as shit for readers too.

Best friends, though, they're the ones that call you out, they shove you out of your comfort zone and thrust you firmly into the "must change" arena.

Sidekicks or BFFs tend to have a specific role. Generally, the sidekick is an "ally" unless you're using the secret-enemy-ally trope, of course. Being an ally means they are a positive support to the hero, though that doesn't mean they're all up in the hero's butt cheeks ass-licking and brown nosing. It means they need to understand the hero's journey and help them get there, even if that requires giving the hero a supportive ass kicking. The BFF-*cum*-sidekick is the most used function and archetype in story, there's always a second in command and this fella is it.

What Friend Sidekicks Do

A friend sidekick's main purpose is to aid the hero. Their job is to help the hero reach the completion of his character arc by having a good ol' chin wag about feelings, brushing Barbie's hair...wait, wrong section. Also, challenging the hero when necessary and, of course, no hero can go on an adventure without their best friend accompanying them on the perilous trip.

Typically, a friend side character will provide one of the following to the plot:

- **Motivation**—be it through problem solving, providing feisty fists up the ass, or being better than the hero. Think Dr. Watson always there to help Sherlock solve the case.
- **Conflict**—through disagreements, bringing information, emotional guilt, or otherwise. Buzz Lightyear brings emotional guilt to Woody in *Toy Story* through their disagreements and Buzz being the kinder of the two characters.
- **Conscience**—showing the hero either through their own actions and values, or through conversations explaining how the hero is being a bit of a twat. Helping the hero to remember their main goal, and pointing out morally questionable behavior, like Janice in *Mean Girls* who tries to show Cady the error of her ways.
- **Companionship**—think Samwise and Frodo. Frodo couldn't have gone to Mordor without him, could he? It's hard to make long trips (be they emotional or physical) on your own.

All of these actions will challenge the hero and push him into doing something. Usually, the side character will do one of two things.

- Express the moral behavior the hero should be demonstrating but can't because he hasn't completed his arc yet—thus guilting the hero into a realization or action.
- Or, on the flip side, expressing the exact opposite

moral behavior thus forcing the hero into action to stop the side character.

The Structural Bits

Allies tend to be major side characters; therefore, they need a crap-ton of page time, origin stories, back stories and mini arcs themselves. These guys should represent the theme in some way. Remember, while the sidekick is here to help aid the protagonist in achieving their goal, they should have their own purpose and life outside of the protagonist too.

Refer back to section 1.3 for more information on major side characters and section 2.2 for how to create characters that represent the theme.

Friendly Mistakes

One core mistake writers often make is thinking the side-kick-friend needs to share similar values to the hero—like both valuing loyalty. They don't. But if you do want your characters to share a similar value, then I urge you—with a very long pointy thing covered in ghost chilis—to consider when constructing your characters, that you need to create different embodiments of their shared value. Take "loyalty" make it different enough so both characters have varying or even polar perspective on any loyalty plot problem that arises. This is so you can create conflict, tension, and keep the pace moving.

How can you do that?

Perhaps hero and friend have different upbringings, a different sense of fashion, different hobbies, different wounds, or different adjoining morals and values. If we take loyalty as a specific example, perhaps the pair finds out a secret about a third mutual friend.

- The hero sees loyalty as telling that third friend the secret.
- But the sidekick sees loyalty as not telling the mutual friend in fear of hurting them.

You, see? Easy peasy.

When the sidekick's views vary from the protagonist's it serves to amplify both of their personality traits through their differences.

The Unlikely Friend

I love this trope...? Tactic...? Tool? Whatever. One of my favorite uses of "the friend" is when a writer creates an unlikely friend character. Why? Because it's unpredictable, baby. And the most interesting characters are the unexpected ones. An ally doesn't have to be an ally from the start. What if the character appeared to be a villain only to turn around and become an ally?

Sometimes these characters start as villains or antagonists before either redeeming themselves, or finding a mutually beneficial goal and thus having to earn the hero's trust and respect, thereby becoming friends.

The Evil Queen, aka Regina in the hit TV show *Once Upon a Time*, is an example of a villain turned friend. Regina's character arc is a redemption arc. She starts out evil and trying to destroy the hero and then sees the error of her ways and gains the trust of Snow White and the Savior eventually, becoming one of the heroes.

Sidekick and Friend Examples

There are a ton of sidekick examples, such as Batman and Robin, Sherlock and Watson. Harry Potter—the greedy fuck—

has approximately eight bazillion friends: Ron, Hermione, Hagrid, Neville, Luna, the list really is endless. In *Lord of the Rings,* Samwise is Frodo's BFF, *Game of Thrones*'s Jon Snow has Ghost the dog, there is Thelma and Louise from the movie of the same name, Pooh and Piglet from A.A. Milne's *Winnie-the-Pooh* books, and Mowgli and Baloo from *The Jungle Book* by Rudyard Kipling. Perhaps one of the more heart-breaking friendships I've ever read comes from *Of Mice and Men* by John Steinbeck, and of course I'm referencing George and Lennie.

5.2 THE GUIDE / MENTOR

Many CEOs and big honchos claim that having a coach or mentor helped them level up during their most impressionable business growth days. And I can't disagree, if you've ever had a power session with a coach, consultant, or mentor, they certainly do help you level up.

That's what the wizened ol' geezer trope "the guide or mentor" function does in a novel.

I don't know about you, but these side characters always make me think of Gandalf or Dumbledore, there's just something about a mentor looking like a shriveled prune with an excess of nasal hair while flinging a knuckled branch of wood around that strikes me as the epitome of mentor. But of course, that's a mistake because not all books are set in the lands of Mordor or Hogwarts. Guides can be in any type of fiction and that's why it's a function.

Why do we need a guide though?

Well, on account of our fine protagonists starting our stories doing a whole lot of stupid shit. But then, that is the point, is it not? A wholly flawed character unable to do the right thing. Too much silly fuckery for you Mr. Protagonist. Let's face it, they don't know any better. In order to learn to use the "force" they need to study and defeat obstacles and of course a guide helps speed up that process by teaching them, "Red saber bad. Other sabers good."*

I should probably point out that while a guide looks like they're there to "prevent" the hero doing stupid shit, they're actually not. Bear with me. See, the hero has to make those mistakes to learn. The mentor is there to tell them not to do the thing so they rebel and go and do precisely that thing and learn their lesson. It's like when your mom tells you if you eat one more cookie you'll puke, so you take a bite because part of you knows the cookies are. Just. So. Yummy... and then you puke an exorcist style fountain of cheesy, acid covered cookie crumbs. You learned your lesson, yo' mama's happy cause she gets to be smug and all "I told you so" and you learn not to eat fifty-six cookies in a row. But if you'd just listened to your mom, it would have been a much more boring story. The hero needs to eat the cookie. Mom needs to tell him not to.

Guides act like parents to the orphaned kids, they act like care givers and family to characters that need it, they happen to represent the teacher-student role too. It's because of this recognizable relationship representation that the guide function is relatable. Most people have had an elder—or just wiser if not older—person care about them and teach them crucial information.

*For the Star Wars pedants, perhaps I should have written "other sabers mostly good." We all know there's a few shades of saber out there, especially in the extended universe. But for the love of Yoda, let me keep the line.

What Guides Do

In *10 Steps to Hero: How to Craft a Kickass Protagonist*, I outline the role of the guide.

"The primary purpose of the guide in a story is threefold: **Teach the hero**, whether that's new skills, new knowledge or otherwise. **Protect the hero** from the villain's devilish party tricks. **Bestow gifts on the hero**, from magical death-wielding weapons to the anecdote that helps the hero have an epiphany."

Many guides will serve all three of these purposes. Giles from *Buffy the Vampire Slayer* is a good example, while he doesn't die as such, he gets knocked out constantly, he teaches her, and bestows magical artifact type gifts.

Within these three core roles, the mentor tends to do some of the following things: Teach the hero new skills (or share knowledge) like Van Helsing teaching Harker all about the effects of garlic and light on vampires in *Dracula*. They guide the way either through training them with the force (nods to Yoda), or physically guides them on the road to Mordor like Gandalf. Often the mentor can provide a little light bashing to the ego, knocking an egomaniac down to size—hello Odin and Thor. Or other times they're role models and consciences like Dexter's father in *Dexter* the TV show. And last, they're often sacrificial lambs like Qui-Gon Jinn and Obi-Wan Kenobi.

When the mentor sacrifices themselves, you'll usually find this happens right around the time the hero is ready to level up —symbolic of the fact the mentor is no longer needed. Gandalf battles the Balrog, although that particular example of sacrifice is contested because he comes back to life. But less contested is half the cast of *Harry Potter* who all make the same sacrifice: Sirius Black, Dumbledore, Lupin, and even Snape in the end. And of course, we just mentioned Obi-Wan Kenobi, who cops it at the end of *Star Wars* so Luke can escape.

The Structural Bits

Guides are likely to be major characters, but less major than the best friend. Purely because the mentor needs to appear, teach or protect, and fuck off back to mentorland again. You may want to sprinkle a little of their backstory in but many mentors simply serve as that, and their background is a mystery or aloof.

There are positive guides and negative guides. The positive guide is your bog-standard mentor, the Dumbledores and Gandalfs of the world, always out for the best interests of the hero and here to help him on his merry way.

The negative guide, though, is not so much here for the hero's good but to drag them into debauchery and chaos— sounds like my kind of fun. These mentors know all the naughty tricks in the book and instead of encouraging the hero down the path to heroism, they spend a chunk of time manipulating the hero and leading them toward darkness, villainy, and morally unacceptable behaviors.

Tyler Durden from *Fight Club* is an amazing example of a negative mentor. Tyler appears to The Narrator during a bout of insomnia and depression. Tyler is a traveling soap salesman who happens to have the same briefcase as The Narrator. Tyler asks The Narrator to hit him and, after some persuasion, The Narrator does. The fist fight provides some relief from the depression, but it's the beginning of a slippery slope that leads to kidnapping The Narrator's girlfriend and blowing up several skyscrapers.

Note that a real hero—i.e., one that is not an antihero or a villain but is also a protagonist—will only go so far down that path. Yes, they might do some bad shit, but ultimately a true hero will avoid crossing the line into villainy.

Guide Mistakes

While the mentor needs to pop in and out of the story, it's a mistake to let that be the only depth you give them. Just like the other side characters, your mentor needs a life outside of the protagonist in order to create depth. It gives you wiggle room to drag the mentor off somewhere "very important" right when your hero needs them most—enabling your hero to grow.

Guide and Mentor Examples

Alfred Pennyworth is Batman's guide, Giles from *Buffy the Vampire Slayer*, Dumbledore from *Harry Potter*, Gandalf from *Lord of the Rings*, Merlin from King Arthur, Haymitch from *The Hunger Games*, the Fairy Godmother from *Cinderella*, Tyrion Lannister from *Game of Thrones*, and Merlin from *The Sword in the Stone*.

Negative Guide Examples

Littlefinger (Lord Petyr Baelish) in *A Song of Ice and Fire* by George R.R. Martin. John Milton in *The Devil's Advocate*, Alonzo in *Training Day*, Gordon Gekko in *Wall Street,* and Tyler Durden in *Fight Club*.

5.3 THE OBSTACLE

Do you ever feel like you're being tested? Let's say you're working on a project in the day job, and it's a biggie. You know as well as your bosses that if you do well in the project, you're going to get promoted. But... your second in command just got sick, there's going to be a three-week delay on the delivery of product you need, and your senior directors just added three more layers of bureaucracy to get through. Without sounding too woo woo–actually who am I kidding this is definitely woo woo—but do you find in life before you can "level up" you end up facing a raft of barriers, problems, or obstacles? I swear this shit happens to me every time I'm about to grow or develop. And the thing is, it needs to happen to your hero too. That is the point of this function.

What Obstacles Do

Obstacles are there to test your hero or heroine and to establish whether or not she's worthy enough to move on to the next step. By "worthy" I mean that she's learned enough about herself and her flaw or the lie she believes. And of course, sometimes that learning is a downward journey before she comes up.

The Structural Bits

Unless you're working on a negative arc, your obstacle functions are unlikely to be villains. These side characters are more likely to be friends testing the hero's values and morals or their aptitude for doing the right thing. They could be mentors testing magical abilities or boxing skill, or henchmen sent to test the protagonist on behalf of the villain.

One of my favorite recent examples of an obstacle comes from the Marvel movie *Black Panther,* in the form of M'Baku. M'Baku is the leader of the Jabari tribe. He opposes T'Challa's —the protagonist and hero's—reign over Wakanda. As T'Challa is about to be crowned, M'Baku challenges him. They fight, but T'Challa wins, earning him the right to be crowned. It marks the beginning of M'Baku's respect for him. Which is why when Eric Killmonger comes to Wakanda and threatens T'Challa, M'Baku sides with T'Challa, saving his life and bringing his armies to help defend him. Thus, the obstacle and challenger becomes an ally.

This challenger turned ally is a common technique found in literature. Snape in some ways is a challenger turned ally—although he also represents several other functions and thus is an example of how side characters can wear many archetype-hats.

Obstacles are like mountains. They should appear throughout your story but with increasing levels of difficulty. The earliest obstacle should be the easiest to defeat; the hero is still a fledging, green around the ears newb, he knows shit-all, so he's not going to be able to defeat some bad ass right-hand man to the villain. No, no, if your story was an intimate love-making session, then these early obstacles are all about the foreplay, darling. You need to tickle and caress the hero's flaws and foibles—we're not spanking and handcuffing him yet, leave the kink for the red room story climax, mkay?

Obstacle Mistakes

Perhaps not a mistake, but more of a missed opportunity. Often the challenges posed to the protagonist are surface-level obstacles. A spell to undo, a question that needs answering, a piece of knowledge that needs finding. But what writers don't always do, is use this as an opportunity to link to the story theme again.

What does this mean? It means rather than posing a generic problem for your hero to overcome, allow your obstacle function to bring something targeted, a problem related to your character's thematic flaw or weakness. This makes the very nature of the test far more powerful because in order to move on, the hero must begin to overcome their flaw. For example, if your theme was about "saving" then perhaps your character has to choose between two things he likes because he can only save one. Or perhaps he has to find a way to save a community project.

Obstacle Examples

The Oracle in *The Matrix,* Fluffy the dog in *Harry Potter,* Sir Didymus, the half-fox, half-terrier guard of the bridge in the movie *The Labyrinth,* Saruman from *Lord of the Rings,* The Winter Soldier in *Captain America,* Roz from *Monsters, Inc.*

5.4 THE HERMES

What Hermes Functions Do

With a short sharp nod to the Greek gods, a Hermes function is the act of bringing and delivering a message. But this isn't any old message. It's a message with such power it results in action and change. Often the messages a Hermes function brings are connected to a plot point, the call to action for the hero or a devastating plot twist.

These messengers are rather crucial motivators to the protagonist. They're like sharp sticks with tasers on the end.

"Hey, Protagonist..."

Pokey, pokey

Insert shocking piece of information

Protagonist leaps into action

You get the point.

The Structural Bits

This is one of the side character's functions that can appear at any level of "sideness." They aren't restricted to major or minor, they can be cameos too. It's worth noting, though, if your Hermes function is a major character then all the trimmings of a major character are required along with it, like personal lives, arcs, and goals.

The messages fall into three categories:

- **Good news,** i.e., help is coming—the Mockingjay in *The Hunger Games*
- **Bad news,** i.e., winter is coming—*Game of Thrones* motif
- **Prophecies,** i.e., Percy Jackson from *Percy Jackson and the Lightning Thief* by Rick Riordan. His prophecy says that the next half-blood child of three specific gods to reach the age of sixteen will make a decision that will either save or destroy Olympus.

In terms of plot, this function can be used to move the plot on, provide a testing piece of information that also forms an obstacle, or shove the hero into the "dark night" if it's a devastating piece of information.

Hermes Mistakes

Perhaps one of the only mistakes with a Hermes function is assuming it needs to be embodied in a person. It does not. In *Cinderella*, for example, the letter invitation she receives to the ball is as much a Hermes character as Professor Trelawny and her prophecies in *Harry Potter*. And while we're discussing a spot of *HP*, another Hermes character, Hedwig the owl—and all the owls in the series for that matter—are Hermes functions in the literal sense, delivering the famous letter calling Harry to Hogwarts.

Hermes Examples

In the original *Matrix* film, the Oracle is both guide, obstacle, and Hermes. Professor Trelawny from *Harry Potter*, Effie in *The Hunger Games,* Hermia in my own book *Keepers*, her name was a nod to Hermes. Bran Stark in *Game of Thrones.*

5.5 SLY FOX

You ever have one of those friends who makes you doubt your very existence? You show them a new outfit and they intentionally hesitate for the briefest of seconds. It's just perceptible enough the doubt seeps into your subconscious and you decide not to wear the outfit after all. Maybe they're more blatant with their disapproval, perhaps they say "mmm nice" instead of "oh my god babe that's fucking gorgeous." There's something malicious about indifference, it really is the killer of confidence.

That's what these functions do. Sometimes you need to knock the hero off their perch. Inserting a sly fox can do that.

What Sly Fox Functions Do

The main purpose of a sly fox is to insert doubt into both the plot, the reader and the hero's psyche.

Why? Because doubt increases tension. If the hero has two paths in front of him and doesn't know which one to take because someone told him bad shit about both, it automatically ramps up the tension because his risk of making a mistake is much higher. Humans in general need to have their questions answered. Doubt creates ambiguity and that means unanswered questions. Readers instantly have a burning need to flip the page and find out what happens next.

This role isn't reserved for choosing the left path or the right one. It's often found in romance stories because it can create doubt about the love interest. But more to the point, this archetype is one of the most flexible of them all. It can be embodied in just about any genre and character type.

The Structural Bits

Like Hermes, Sly Fox functions can appear in any side character—major, minor or in between. With all these functions you need to create the right amount of depth and roundness according to whichever level of side character you choose.

Sly foxes are usually seen earlier in the plot because the hero is more susceptible to misinformation as they haven't defeated their flaw and therefore are naiver and more gullible. It would be unusual to find a sly fox still able to influence a hero once the hero has gone through the "dark night," i.e., the point at which he finds the final piece of the puzzle in order to defeat the villain.

Sly foxes come in two variants: positive and negative.

A **positive** sly fox will still appear to cast doubt early in the book but, by the end, they are allies, anti-heroes, lovers, or other "good" characters.

This is most common in romance stories where the love interest is often a sly fox. In these plots, the protagonist tends to (because of their flaw) deem her love interest's behavior as erratic or fickle and this creates doubt over his real feelings for her. This uncertainty then creates psychological or moral barriers in the protagonist's mind. Until they're overcome the characters can't get together.

A **negative** sly fox casts doubt early on like the positive sly fox. But, that's where the similarity ends. These negative ninnies are bad for a good reason. These fellas turn out to have ulterior motives, dark sides and/or are out to attack the hero. For example, Glenn Close plays Alex Forrest in *Fatal Attraction*. She's an example of a negative sly fox, turning from a perfect lover into a sadistic killer.

Sly Fox Mistakes

There's only one mistake you need to watch out for with the sly fox function, and that's not revealing their true nature.

If you have a sly fox interfering with the plot, then you need to make sure you resolve this thread by allowing the protagonist to call them out and uncover their deception—just like in *Fatal Attraction*, it would be an odd film otherwise. Not doing this leaves the thread hanging and the reader feeling like there's no comeuppance for the wrong doer. Even in a positive sly fox, the thread still needs resolving or the lovers can't get together and we all know how vicious a romance reader will get if you don't give them a happily ever after. Do yourself a favor and resolve the thread.

Sly Fox Examples

Keyser Soze from *The Usual Suspects*, appears as a disabled gentleman throughout the entire film until the end, where his true nature as the perpetrator is revealed. Nikolai Lantsov from Leigh Bardugo's *Grisha* series appears for the first half of *Siege and Storm* (book 2 in the series) as one character, but his true nature as a prince isn't revealed until a crucial point in the book.

Other examples of sly foxes include Scar from *The Lion King,* who makes Simba believe his dad's death was his fault;

Dr. Elsa Schneider from *Indiana Jones* and Prince Hans from the Disney movie *Frozen*.

5.6 THE JOKER

I'd love to whip out a court jester outfit and write this section dressed in my best joker outfit, that or paint my face white, dye my hair green, and whip a knife across my smile. But none of those things are quite right.

This function is a mood lightener. Which is why it doesn't always have to be embodied in a character, but can be a thing, an event, or any other delicious little bite of comedy you can concoct. You know how every friendship group has one diva? The guy or gal who's cutting banter is so on point it makes you drool as they slice down egos and bitch slap dickheads? Those guys are the joker. They're mischievous, playful, and bring a bit of fun to the story.

What Joker Functions Do

But they actually do more than just have excellent dialogue. In symbolic terms, the joker represents the need for change. Banter is a subtle nudge to the receiving character to "sort their shit out." Think of the movie *When Harry Met Sally,* she cuts him down, mocking him for thinking women don't fake orgasms, in one of the most brilliant movie take downs I've ever watched.

While these characters revel in the banter, there's often something meaningful behind the quippy wit. Their wit can call attention to hypocrisy, deceptions, and dishonesty.

The Structural Bits

Jokers can be major characters and play a significant role in your story, but in most circumstances they don't change. Meaning they're flat characters without an arc. Of course, when you have a character like The Grinch who is a joker *and* the protagonist, that's not going to be the case. Donkey from *Shrek* is another joker character with a character arc. But for the vast majority of characters who are "jokers" they're going to have a flat character arc. They'll stick rigidly to their embodiment of the theme whether that's positive or negative.

In terms of plot impact, these characters serve as the catalyst for change in other characters. They do this by drawing subtle attention and pressure to the wrongness in the hero's— or other character's—world.

Joker Mistakes

If your jokers are side characters, then under most circumstances allowing them to change or develop through an arc could be a mistake, as would letting them flip flop on the theme. But like I always say, "rules can be broken."

Joker Examples

Other examples of jokers include Timon and Pumba from

The Lion King, Loki from both the mythology and the Marvel movies. Dobby the house elf from *Harry Potter*, *The Grinch*, and *The Cat in the Hat*, created by Dr Seuss or Merry and Pippin from *Lord of the Rings*, Odin and Loki from *American Gods* by Neil Gaiman, and the Artful Dodger from *Oliver Twist*, Olaf from *Frozen*, and Donkey from *Shrek*.

5.7 THE WORLD

This might surprise you, but the world—as in your story world —can be used as a side character. It's an interesting, if a little unexpected, choice for character creation because of course it's not embodied in a person—under most circumstances. The world—your world—especially in fantasy, science fiction, or any genre where you have an ability to make changes to the world, can make for a character in and of itself.

I get giddy and hand-flappy when I start worldbuilding. I know it can be hard for some, it's one of the most magical parts of being an author. I still remember reading as a kid and being in physical roll-around-the-floor-whining pain because I couldn't visit the rich world an author had created. Isn't that just the most spectacular skill? Not only do we get to lie and make shit up for a living, we literally create new universes that kids and adults inhabit so much they wish they were real.

Many writers focus on plot and character as the two most important factors of a story, but lest we forget setting is a very close third. The setting is the world in which your characters inhabit and the location in which the plot occurs. It's a vital part of your book, and so spending a little time and thought on it is essential—even if you're basing your story in the "real" world. Why? Because for those authors that do setting well, it creates another emotional layer for your readers to connect to. I'm sure readers of non-fantasy genres have longed to visit the mansion where a historical romance was set, or central London because an urban fantasy story was set there. Well-created settings connect with readers and that serves to deepen the story and the link with a reader's emotions.

Key questions to think about are:

- What are your main story locations?
- Do any of those locations repeat, i.e., do your characters inhabit those locations multiple times?
- What are the main characteristics of your setting?
- Can any of these characteristics create conflict or support a plot point?

Don't Be Afraid to Chip Chop, Snip Snap

Occasionally we can get locked into a way of thinking. We decide that something occurs in a certain location and that's the end of it, thank you very much. While our prose changes during the edits, the locations often don't.

And yet, three times now, I've had to change the location a scene was set in order for the book to work. For me, all of these scenes were the opening chapter. While the "plot" in that scene stayed relatively stable, the actual setting changed. By changing the location, it enabled the plot to move faster and mesh with the other scenes more effectively. Originally, *Victor*, book two, was going to start in Eden's open home tower before the start of term. However, the opening felt stagnant and sluggish. I couldn't seem to get the characters to the university location I needed. So, I rolled the story on a bit and set the opening at the train station as the characters were arriving and then I wove in the conversations they had in the original scene.

If one of your scenes isn't working, don't be afraid to change location. It's always worth asking yourself what would happen to the plot and characters if you moved a scene to a different location because the story-world matters.

Recurring Settings

If your characters are off on a voyage where they won't have a recurring setting at all, then feel free to ignore this section. For anyone that does have a recurring setting, then it's time to consider the locations that repeat. Just like the importance of a side character changes with their frequency on the page, so too does the setting. The more a setting is used, the more important it is and the more depth it should have.

The House in the Cerulean Sea by T.J. Klune is predominantly set on Marsyas island. A small island set in the Cerulean Sea, with one large mansion style house on it. A house where all the side characters live. This island provides the setting for about 50–60% of the story. Thus, the details and quirks included are phenomenal and bring the story alive. Each character has their own room and each room is unique. One quirk is that the island itself has a sprite creature that protects it, and in a way, embodies the island's personality. Strange and magical things happen on the island, adventures in the forest, it's always sunny there—a direct contrast to the opening location which is a miserable, gray, and rainy city where Linus, the protagonist, lives. I suspect this was a deliberate juxtaposition to demonstrate how wonderful the island was in comparison to Linus' home city. You, see? The world matters.

The Structural Bits

Rather than creating info dumps about your world, you can use your side characters to reveal expository pieces of information. For example, if your characters are in conversation and they reveal past details about a school or an event that happened, you remove the blatant exposition because they're talking about it in reference to their own experience.

You can use the nature of the world to create obstacles and barriers for your characters. For example, use the weather to make it difficult for your characters to reach their destination. Make the terrain or land treacherous to cross, with big hills or ravines with no way to cross. Make it rain when they need it to be sunny.

Of course, this works the other way around. In *Six of Crows*, Inej is climbing up an incinerator pipe—the incinerator is on, I should add—and her rubber soled shoes begin to melt as she's still twenty feet from the top. If it weren't for the skies opening and shedding a load of droplets on her, she'd have fallen to her death. You can see that the world can shower your characters with gifts and help or be a treacherous git and make their lives difficult.

Questions to ask:

- How does the world push back against the main character's wants and needs?
- How is the protagonist at odds with the world?
- How has the world shaped the protagonist?

AIDAN and Personification

In the book *Illuminae* by Jay Kristoff and Amie Kaufman, Kady—the protagonist—spends 95% of the story on a space-ship. Which means the spaceship is her world. This particular spaceship-world is sentient of sorts. Personification on steroids if you like. The spaceship is embodied by a disembodied Artificial Intelligence called AIDAN... I know, it's a bit to wrap your head around, but it's an excellent example of how you can create a world that causes carnage for your characters. It's a fantastic example of personifying your world too.

In *An Unkindness of Magicians*, Kat Howard bases her magician's world around the houses the magicians live in. Each house has a personality and can refuse you entry or make your life difficult. While there are a variety of these houses and therefore, they're not as all-encompassing as AIDAN, they are reoccurring locations and locations the characters spend a significant portion of time in and thus, part of the world.

Another couple of examples include The Capitol from *The Hunger Games* by Suzanne Collins. The Capitol and districts are distinctly unique settings because of the glamour and wealth in The Capitol and the grades of poverty in the rest of the districts. But The Capitol is an awesome example for more than just the quirky glamour, it's the overarching and intangible villain, albeit it is symbolically represented through President Snow.

Hogwarts, the school in *Harry Potter*, is another example of a world with character. The school is alive in a sense as a character. It has moving staircases and portrait paintings that speak.

World Personality

If you treat your world as a character then arguably because of the size of its role in the story it would be a "major" character. This means you likely need backstory and an arc of some kind. Of course, this isn't compulsory, you're not going to ruin your story by not having a character arc for your world. But here are some things to consider:

World Backstory

Backstory helps shape personality. While you don't need a year-by-year breakdown of the last one thousand years of history, if there are key events that have happened that either affect the characters directly in your novel, or that have had a generational impact, or perhaps play some role in shaping a more realistic world, then there's no harm in including them at the right point in your story.

For example, there were three major wars in my Eden East series, the consequence of one particular war between Mermaids and Sirens is still having an impact in the current plot. This war is referenced and explained. However, one of the other wars, named "the West War" is not relevant to the current plot. While I—as the author—know the details of what happened and why, it's just a random piece of worldbuilding that came to me and therefore I've not included it in any of the books as it's not impacting the current timeline.

Character Arcs

If you're writing a contemporary romance, then your setting might not change, unless it's set in a bookstore that's being closed, for example. However, for those where the world *can* change, it's worth considering whether or not you want to include a change. Now, before we get silly, this doesn't mean you start making your roads speak as "gravelly" phone sex workers, or your weather strip naked and vanish—unless that's a thing in your fantasy world. But in most dystopian books, for example, you have a certain amount of destruction occur; this changes the world. Battles and wars will ravage areas of your world and that should leave a lasting mark. You'll want to consider how these changes either help or hinder your characters and your story plot. Can you make it work for you and create conflict? What if there's only one bridge across a ravine and an earthquake collapses it? Uh-oh spaghetti O, protagonists in a world of oopsies now.

You can use the world changing symbolically to represent what's really happening. For example, in my Eden East series, each location has a specific type of weather, such that in one location it's always winter, in another it's monsoon-like. These locations are separated—just as the world is, a consequence of an historical event. When the plants and greenery start dying, it worries the characters because it's a sign that their ecosystem is failing. But the subtext is symbolizing the imminent destruction of their world.

If it's not physical damage or change to your world by the villain, then perhaps your characters are the ones who have changed and see the world differently now? I don't know whether you've ever gone back and visited your first school, but I remember when—as an adult—I drove past the first school I went to. I was shocked at how small the playground was, how tiny the buildings were. Everything had seemed bigger when I was four years old. Perceptions change, people change, worlds change.

Sourcing Inspiration

Inspiration for worldbuilding comes from everywhere, but if you're feeling stuck then here are some suggestions for where you can research locations:

- Start with your local area. Are there any myths or historical stories surrounding buildings or locations in your local area?
- Look to stately homes, large mansions or celebrity houses for ideas for larger locations.
- If you don't want to use famous locations, look to

retail parks, shopping centers, museums, university
campuses, or large schools.

- Other things you can research include nature
  reserves, odd architecture, and what of larger
  transportation like cruise ships or jumbo jets?
- Consider websites like the Atlas Obscura, which
  have a wealth of quirky and unusual locations that
  can be used as spring boards for creating new
  worlds.

Using the Senses

The world is a sensory place. To make your world's character as full and in-depth as possible you need to engage the
senses. Unlike other side characters, your world doesn't get
dialogue or emotions. In the real world, we as humans interact
with our environment through our senses. We touch surfaces,
hear nature, feel the weather, see cities, taste food. One of the
fastest ways to build your world and to make it feel alive is to
use the senses. Let your characters interact with and feel the
world. And don't just pick one sense. Layer the senses. We
rarely see the senses used in isolation. If you're hearing leaves
and branches crackle, you're probably seeing a forest or field. If
you're tasting potatoes, you're probably smelling meat or warm
vegetables too. Consider using more than one sense when you
start to build your world.

Be deliberate about your use of the senses. For example,
you could connect the scent a character is smelling to the
theme in your book, to foreshadowing, or to subtly hint at
symbolism.

If you want to learn more about using the senses in your
writing, I've published a course on using the senses in prose
which you can find here: sachablack.co.uk/senses

How Do You Give Your World Character?

Angeline Trevena—author of Dystopian Urban Fantasy, Post-Apocalyptic Fiction, and nonfiction for authors—has written a multitude of worldbuilding books for writers, such as *30 Days of Worldbuilding*. Find out more about Angeline on her website: angelinetrevena.co.uk. I asked Angeline for her top tips on using the world as a character. You can find her world-building books in the recommended reading section.

Angeline says:

"You can use your setting in the same ways you use your various characters, whether you're creating a fictional setting, or using a real-world location. It can push the plot forward, raise the stakes, and even become the antagonist. So much more than a wishy-washy backdrop.

So, how do we do this?

Match your genre. To really give your setting a feel of belonging, like your story couldn't have taken place anywhere else, match it to the genre of your book. You can have flowing fields, mysterious mountains, and stretching seas in your epic fantasy. You can have a rusty scavenger's paradise in your post-apocalyptic novel. Of course, you can play with this, and turn it on its head. If you want to set your gritty urban fantasy in a sunny chocolate-box village then do so. But make sure the village has a dark side to discover; smuggler's caves, underground tombs, a nearby forest where it really feels like you're being watched.

Match your themes. In the same way that your characters explore and reveal your book's themes, your setting can do this too. If secrets are a theme, include hidden rooms, or unmapped countries. If coming of age is a theme, let your setting mature with your characters as they ditch the local arcade for a more sophisticated coffee shop. If you're exploring redemption, let's see the old slave market demolished and a garden of unity planted instead.

Use the history. Whether you're creating a fictional location, or using a real-world setting, you can use the history of that place. What's that memorial for, and how can you tie it into your story? Who's buried in the local graveyard? How did that building burn down, and what has replaced it? Look for unusual historical events or people, hidden histories, or histories that have been erased.

What's it like to live there? Really get to know your location in the same way your characters would, and remember that a resident will have a very different experience of a place than a tourist or visitor will. Where are the bad parts of town? How do your characters get around? What places are they ashamed of, and what makes them proud? Remember, also, to use all of the senses: think about what a place smells like, or sounds like. Perhaps the local bread factory only fires up on Tuesdays, or the local farmers fertilize their fields at the weekend. Just as your characters have their own individual mix of traits, so does your setting. Look for the little details to make the place distinct and unique.

Do your research! If you're using a real-world setting, even if you're adapting it with fictional elements, make sure you do your research. Know which buses go where, know which day the record shop shuts early, know which church clock chimes 30 seconds before the others. For any readers who know the location, they will love you for getting these details right! And for people who don't know it, your attention to detail makes it all the more real.

Give it a reputation. We all know that reputations are easy to gain, and much harder to lose! What reputation does your setting have, and how has it gained it? We associate different places with different sentiments. If you're planning a romantic holiday, you're likely to think of Paris or Rome. You're less likely to consider Salem, Pendle Hill, or Stephen King's Derry. Of course, you might, if you're so inclined! Think about how the reputation of your location is perpetuated: through urban legends, socio-economics and population demographics, as well as the physical appearance and location. A run-down town living under the constant shadow of a mountain may have a very different reputation to its tidier neighbor in the sunny pasture.

Give it a character arc and journey. Your location can develop and grow, just as your character does. A place can be redeveloped, or become wealthier. Likewise, it can befall a disaster and become a ghost town. As your character proceeds on their journey, perhaps the city they once felt so safe in becomes sinister and unfamiliar. By giving the setting an arc of its own, you can increase your character's tension, and raise the stakes for them. Your location can begin to cause conflict with increased riots, or a new oppressive government, or by closing down the magic academy. Or, it can help your character towards their goal, or it can even provide the inciting incident that kicks off your whole story.

Love the place! Fall in love with your setting, even if it's a terrifying place that you would never choose to live yourself! Let your passion for your setting come through in your writing, and let your readers really care about it, just as they care for your characters."

STEP 5 SIDE CHARACTER FUNCTIONS SUMMARY

- In which we brushed Barbie's hair, sent messages via gods, saw the world in a new light, and peppered the hero's path with obstacles.

Major archetypes include:

- The Friend
- The Guide
- The Obstacle
- Hermes
- Sly Fox
- The Joker
- The World

- Friends provide motivation, conflict, conscience, and companionship. Friends tend to be major side characters with arcs and a lot of page time. Don't make the mistake of thinking they need to be similar to the hero, they don't.

- The guide always makes me think of a slew of old beardy wizards! The guide and mentor's primary purpose is to: teach the hero, protect the hero or bestow gifts on them. Guides can be positive or negative.
- Obstacles are the testers of your hero, has he leveled up yet? Good, you may move on. While these guys are there to test the hero, they're unlikely to be the actual villain. Try to make your obstacles about the theme and your hero's flaw.
- Hermes functions are the harbingers of information, messages, omens, prophecies, and more. Some messages are positive, others negative, and don't assume it has to be embodied in a character; message functions are letters and owls and invitations too!
- Sly foxes are insidious little nasties, created to make the protagonist doubt the very fiber of their being. These fellas tend to be found earlier in the book, and they can represent as positive or negative characters. One thing you must always do with a sly fox is reveal their true nature and any underhand activities they've been involved with.
- Jokers are the "fun" in any story. Their job is to lighten the mood, bring a smile to the reader and to the other characters; but don't forget that sometimes, under humor is a layer of truth or meaning that can draw the protagonist's attention to areas they need to work on. These fellows are often —but not always—flat characters without arcs; in order to keep their humorous side, they stay as they are.

The world is the often-forgotten character in a book, but it's vital to creating a real world for your characters to inhabit. Questions to ask yourself:

- What are your key story locations?
- Do any of those locations repeat, i.e., do your characters inhabit those locations multiple times?
- What are the main characteristics of your setting?
- Can any of these characteristics create conflict or support a plot point?
- How does the world push back against the main character's wants and needs?
- How is the protagonist at odds with the world?
- How has the world shaped the protagonist?

- Remember, your world can have a personality as much as your other characters. Create an arc for it or a backstory or a reputation.

Questions to Think About

1. Note down a list of worlds from your genre, what elements make them stand out?
2. Can you identify one of each archetype from books in the genre you write in?

STEP 6 ARC WEAVING

6.0 ARC WEAVING

Where we beat our characters, have sister-lovers, change, grow and then fall, and arc it deeper, bitch.

Spoiler warning movies: *Mean Girls, Toy Story, Lord of the Rings*

Spoiler warning TV shows: *Once Upon a Time, Breaking Bad, Game of Thrones*

Character arcs are often associated solely with the protagonist of a story. That's because heroes are flop-your-dick-out flashy and their arc takes center stage as the most significant arc in any story. By definition, a character arc is the change your protagonist (or other character) undergoes during a story. It's the take-a-scalpel-to-the-chest, slice the hero open, and mash your fist around until you find the inner journey they're going on.

Stories are about change, and this "arc" is the representation of that change. The arc will begin at the start of your story with your character flawed and end with them as a different version of themselves because of the experiences they have in your novel.

Every author knows their hero needs to experience this change. But what of side characters? In Step 1 we covered the fact that cameos and minor characters don't need arcs. But major side characters do. So what the fucknuts do we do about them?

They can't have the same amount of page time as the protagonist—our books would be so big they'd intimidate Kilimanjaro.

One of the purposes of a side character is to either aid or block the hero's goal and arc. But before we dive into side character arcs specifically, let's look at what arcs are. Generally speaking, there are three main types of arc: positive, negative, and flat.

Positive Arc

A positive arc is the most common type of character arc in both genre fiction and film. Especially for protagonists. When talking about the protagonist, they'll begin with some major flaw or personality issue that stops them from growing and developing and defeating the villain. When referring to major side characters, the same principles apply. Major side characters begin flawed and that flaw prevents them from achieving their goal or defeating their personal villain. It won't be the main story villain, of course; those bad boys are reserved for the hero.

Throughout the story, your major side character will encounter an obstacle (or obstacles depending on how big of a character they are and how large their subplot is) that will change them for the better, enlighten them, and give them the strength they need to defeat their personal villain. These side characters will end the story in a better place than they started it.

A positive arc can take many forms from growth, healing, and self-discovery, and usually results in happy story endings. Which is why they are commonly found in romance, young adult, and children's stories.

Ron Weasley and Neville Longbottom from *Harry Potter* are great examples of this. Both side characters start the series unconfident and end it confident and fearless. Neville beheads Voldemort's snake Nagini after pulling the Gryffindor sword out of the hat and Ron ends up with the girl of his dreams.

Negative Arc

A negative arc is the opposite of a positive character arc. If we're talking heroes then they will end the novel in a worse position than they started. Likewise for side characters. As villains are often classed as side characters, this is the most common form of arc for a villain.*

Instead of experiencing a journey of change and enlightenment, a character experiencing a negative arc will slide into villainy, darkness, or a negative portrayal of their personality traits in whatever form that takes. The negative arc can be portrayed in a variety of delicious and devious ways from a corrupt character to a disillusioned one. While there are always examples of villains with negative arcs, there are fewer heroes or side characters with this arc. Having side characters that embody negative representations of the theme help the protagonist to process and work out how to answer your story's question. That means you don't have to limit negative representations of the theme to just the villain.

Some examples of characters with negative arcs are: Michael Corleone from *The Godfather* by Mario Puzo, Dorian from *The Picture of Dorian Gray* by Oscar Wilde, Walter White from *Breaking Bad*, and Cersei Lannister from *A Song of Fire and Ice* by George R.R. Martin.

*If a villain were to have a positive arc, this is called a "redemption arc." One of the more recent examples I've seen of this is Regina the Evil Queen in the TV show *Once Upon a Time*.

Flat Arc

A flat arc means your protagonist or side character starts your novel more or less fully formed. In this instance, your story is less about the change your character undergoes and more about the change they invoke in the story or world. This is true for side characters too. Often there is a side character who embodies a positive representation (or sometimes negative) of the theme and remains steadfast to that representation. Think of the BFF who is a good friend throughout the plot. Inevitably the hero hurts them at some point in the story but like a good ickle, wittle BFF, they accept them back and continue on being a good friend. A good example of this is Janis from *Mean Girls*. Cady hurts Janis when she behaves like a dick. Janis tries to be a good friend by attempting to warn Cady and show her she's being a bellend, but Cady ignores her until she learns her lesson. And Janis? Well, because she's a good friend she forgives Cady and they all live happily ever after.

Unlike the other arcs where the story acts upon the hero, in this arc the hero (or in our case, side character) doesn't change. The novel is driven by the changes the character creates. This structure is most often seen with anti-heroes or serial stories like crime novels or mysteries — think Sherlock Holmes. Katniss Everdeen from *The Hunger Games* has a flat arc as she doesn't change herself so much as change the dystopian world around her. Likewise with side characters. Although their job isn't usually to act upon the world—that's the protagonist's duty as the one with the biggest impact on the story—the side character's role is to affect the hero. The change a side character with a flat arc creates is to show the hero the error of their ways or their thinking. Which these characters do quite literally by maintaining their arc/status/opinion. Janis is always a good friend, and it's one of the nudges Cady needs to help her see she was behaving like a flaccid penis. A few more examples include James Bond, Indiana Jones, and Jack Reacher.

Give 'em a Beating

One thing all readers share in common is a heartfelt solidarity for a character going through shit times. Which means you have an excellent tool at your disposal. Everyone knows you need to push your protagonist into precarious situations, and make them face obstacles and/or problems. You need to push them further and further into a hole before you haul them out into the light.

Now, we know there's a finite number of pages you can give your side characters. But for the characters who frequent the pages more often, you can sprinkle—and I don't mean liberally, I mean a tight-fisted dash of a sentence or two—some character beatings in.

Just like your hero, your side characters should have to work for their goals. Beat them down, make it hard for them to attain their deepest desires, it makes riveting tension and grips readers to the page.

Buzz Lightyear goes through a depression of sorts after he discovers he's not, in fact, a real space ranger. And yet, by the end of the story, his faith is restored in himself and he believes even more ardently that he's capable of anything. But he had to work for that belief.

Victim of Our Own Choices

This harks back to the equation I mentioned earlier. E + R = O. Event plus reaction equals outcome. That should be the case for your hero and it should be the case for your side characters too.

The crap your protagonist lands in should be as a direct consequence of whatever nonsense decision they've made. Likewise with your side characters, any beating or difficulties they experience should be as a result of their own choices in trying to reach their goals. Or perhaps even because they don't want to follow the protagonist or disagree with their decisions.

6.1 CHANGE ARCS, GROWTH ARCS, AND FALL ARCS

Okay, we know there's a positive arc, negative arc, and a flat arc. But within those arcs, what variations do we have?

Three of the most common arcs are: change arc, growth arc, and a fall arc. Let's take them arc by arc.

Change Arcs

This is understandably the most common form of arc as changing gives the starkest growth on a hero's flaw. Thor has a change arc—he was self-indulgent and self-obsessed at the start of the Marvel movie and in order to regain his hammer, he has to learn to become humble and serve his people. This is a dramatic change of personality. Side character Hermione Granger from the *Harry Potter* series undergoes a similar change from bossy know it all to humble, helpful, and altogether less irritating. Luke Skywalker from *Star Wars* is another example of a radically changing character.

One key factor in this type of arc is that the character needs to be changing from something to something. The easiest representation of this is to create a lie the character believes.

Like Hermione who believes "being knowledgeable is more important than anything." She quickly realizes friendship is more important and the lie she believes is eradicated.

But it doesn't have to be a hardcore lie, it could be a misperception, a myth, or misunderstanding.

The other key factor is that your character must—as the name of the arc suggests—change. Their personality can't stay the same else they're undergoing a growth arc instead of a change arc.

These types of arcs are generally reserved for the protagonist because the change is so dramatic and transformational it's hard to depict it comprehensively without the page time a protagonist gets. That's not to say it can't be done of course, need I mention there are no rules?

THERE ARE NO RULES.

If you're writing a long-running series then your major side characters have more page space to undergo change arcs through the books.

Growth Arcs

While growth arcs are similar to change arcs because they both provide a change of some kind, the change in a growth arc is less radical. Change arcs are total transformations. Growth arcs are... well, growth! The character's initial personality remains intact, they just become a better, more rounded version of themselves by the end of the story.

What you typically see in a novel is the protagonist in a story having a change arc and then the side characters having growth arcs. The fact that growth arcs are less dramatic also serves to highlight just *how* dramatic of a change the protagonist goes through.

What does a growth arc look like? Typically, they present in one of a variety of forms:

- Learning something new (like the truth about a lie they believed)
- Changing their perspective
- Having a different role in life, their job, their family etc

Jamie Lannister in the *Game of Thrones* series is a great example of this. He grows and learns and becomes mildly better than he was at the start, but ultimately ends up in the same place he started—with his sister-lover. Another example I mentioned earlier is Buzz Lightyear, who starts out believing he can do anything because he's a space ranger and ultimately, he ends the story still believing he can do anything. But at the end, he is more rounded as a character because he knows the truth about his identity. For Buzz, it's a new perspective on an old belief. Samwise Gamgee from *Lord of The Rings* has a growth arc, unlike Frodo who's irrevocably changed, Samwise is older, slightly more haggard and a little wiser than at the start of the books.

This type of arc is what's used most often for side characters. Why? Because there's a less dramatic shift in the character, it doesn't require quite as much page time to depict—although that's not to say this is a shallow arc to choose. Not at all, you can still deep dive into this type of arc across a novel if you show enough of the change.

The most important aspect of a growth arc is that at the end of the book, they are still the same person in their soul as they were at the beginning of the journey.

The second most important aspect is that you can put your finger on a tangible aspect of growth be that an improvement, opinion shift, lesson learned etc.

Fall Arc

This represents a negative arc. As the name suggests, this is a character who falls or declines. They make bad choices, shit goes bad, and in the end, they doom themselves to failure. Most often, it's the poor neglected villain who goes through this arc. Though of course, heroes can have fall arcs, as can side characters.

The most common outcome of this type of arc is death. That can be a literal or figurative death. Literal death is obvious, but a figurative death could be the death of a fundamental part of their personality, the death of their morality or something else. See Step 7 for more on side character death.

Other outcomes include corruption, insanity, imprisonment, disillusionment or any other devastating incident you fancy. Something to note about this type of arc in particular is that, usually, the character damages themselves as well as those around them. This is something to think about in terms of conflict and consequence of the side character's actions. What are the implications for the protagonist? Can you use this to drive the plot on or throw an obstacle at the hero?

While this type of arc is most commonly found in the villain, it's not isolated to the villain. For example, Walter White, the protagonist from the TV show *Breaking Bad*, is a fantastic example of a protagonist with a fall arc. Dorian Gray from *The Picture of Dorian Gray* is another protagonist with a fall arc. Cersei Lannister and Sansa Stark are two examples of characters with fall arcs from the *Game of Thrones* series. Cersei is a classic fall arc. However, Sansa is an interesting case, because while she falls from her "innocence" at the start of the series, she also rises to power and it's somewhat of an empowerment for her—which is positive for the lass!

Fall arcs, while mostly used with villains, can be extremely powerful if used on a character who starts the story as "good" and moral. It's for that reason that I like Sansa's fall arc more than Cersei's. Cersei was bad to the bone from the start, which is why her arc is more of a growth-fall, as opposed to a pure fall arc.

If you're stuck with your side characters and need to bring them to life, then consider how these types of arc could help you deepen their characters and how you can interconnect them to the protagonist.

6.2 WHO'S WHO IN THE GREAT ARC STAKES?

There is a commonality between protagonists and their counterparts. One of the fastest ways to make a side character real to the reader is for them to want something, and in fact, it's a vital part of their character arc.

Teachers often talk about the hero's burning desire for whatever their goal is, but that doesn't mean the side character should have a desire that's less potent than the protagonist's. Oh no, we all frolic in the desire pit, darlings. Don't be selfish with the goal lust. Side characters can partake of this poison too. The difference, though, is that it's not the side character's story. As much as they might burn for their goal in the same tingly way, they'll never get the same page time to explore it fully. The majority of it has to happen off page.

The key is that, where the side character and protagonist's goals intersect, or where one can impact the other, create conflict, tension or an obstacle, then let those scenes spill over the page. In these cases, it will serve the larger plot purpose—and that's a good thing.

How Do You Know Who Needs What Arc?

In the earlier chapter "WTF Is a Side Character Anyway?" we identified the three main types of side character: cameo, minor, and major.

The first two—cameos and minor characters—are unlikely to have character arcs.

Why?

Because changing takes time, and in a book, time equals page count. Unfortunately for these unloved little munchkins page time is not something they get much of. But that's okay, someone has to play the bit-parts. It means they get to be flatter, unchanging, and in some ways more of a caricature of a character, rather than a fully fleshed-out fictional one.

The side characters that do need an arc are your major side characters. Note here I'm not saying *all* your major side characters need arcs, but the most significant characters do—the ones who both influence the protagonist or directly affect the plot will need more than just a two-dimensional appearance.

So then, how do you know if your characters need a fuller arc or just the impression of an arc? Here are some good questions to ask yourself:

- **Does your character appear three times or less?** If yes, do not pass go, do not collect $200 and definitely do not give them an arc.
- **Does your character have sufficient impact on the plot that they change, influence or sway the protagonist or a storyline?** If not, see above, these babes don't need shit other than a cheeky tap on the bum and a fiver in their character-bra. If yes, then ask yourself the next question...
- **Are they one of your main characters best mates, a very key player or appear in the majority of scenes?** If yes, they probably need a character arc or at least the impression of one.

What Do All Arcs Need?

The basic requirements for any character arc are:

- Needing or wanting something
- Not being able to get said thing
- Changing or doing something in order to...
- Get the thing!

Just like your protagonist—you see how much of the set-up is the same? By the end of the book, they either need to have gotten whatever they desired, realized they didn't want it anyway, or not been able to achieve their goal.

There's another key point about the arcs. Whatever the side character "wants" needs to be relevant to the plot. If you're writing an arctic-based husky racing story, it's no good the side characters wanting to enter the pie baking championships. What relevance is that to the story? How does it add anything? It doesn't.

Showing a Side Character Arc

The difference between a protagonist arc and a side character then, is that we—the reader—may only see points one and four of a side character arc: the want and getting it. Points two and three may be alluded to, referenced in conversation or via flashback or not at all. Of course, that isn't a rule, with some major side characters you will see all four points albeit in much less detail than a protagonist.

But the easiest way of creating a small arc is to show the beginning and the end only.

A word of caution though: if you present a side character one way at the start of your book and then another way at the end, while it creates the sense of an arc, simply presenting the side character one way and then another, without any explanation or justification, will make some readers feel hard done by. It could also make your characters flat and unrealistic.

How then, do you combat that problem?

It doesn't take much to suggest or imply a change in a character. If a conversation happened at the start of your story about marriage and getting engaged and the character was adamant on never getting married, then your protagonist—and reader—should experience one or two additional conversations where they see that opinion and mindset start and then fully shift.

How do humans indicate a change of opinion?

- Our voice, tone, and words change
- Our posture and subconscious body language changes
- Our mindset shifts
- Our actions change

You can use all of these as indicators in your story that your characters changed.

Yes, you absolutely can just flip how a character is feeling. You can have a minor character say they hate marriage at the start of your story and then have the traitorous mongrel engaged at the end. But what's more effective is to give your reader the reason why. Show them what nudged your character into changing their mind.

If your side character is important enough, i.e., they are a reflection of the story theme, then try and tie in one of the plot obstacles or conflict situations into their arc as well as an indication of why they're changing.

Hero Arcs Versus Side Character Arcs

Your hero's arc is the representation of the book's theme. Obviously, that could be a negative arc or a flat one. But for simplicity and the fact the majority of hero arcs are positive, let's assume it's a positive arc. This means, then, that the villain or antagonist will have the opposite arc. And your side characters will have arcs that represent various shades of the positivity or negativity in-between.

Does your hero start out the lonely orphan kid unable to connect and then become surrounded by family and loved ones by the end? Cool, your antagonist needs to start out the opposite—super popular and surrounded by adoring people. But that means the villain needs to end the book in the opposite state: alone, friendless with family hating on them. This would create a negative arc and beautiful diametric representation of the theme.

Where does that leave your side characters? Well, one example would be to represent a character with a flat arc, someone who stays the same throughout the story. Perhaps they're a moderately popular kid, not a total dong, and therefore they treat people and their friends nicely and continue to do so throughout the story, representing some aspect of "how to be a good friend" that the hero needs to see and learn from in order to change.

What does a character arc look like for a side character? Their arc needs to be smaller than the hero's so that it doesn't take over the story. Which means they won't ever get a fully explored arc in the same way the protagonist does.

With a protagonist, you explore *on page* every aspect and every moment of their arc and change. We see them before they change, we see the journey of their change, what influences them to change, the thinking they did in order to accept the change as well as what happens after the change.

But you simply don't have time for every character to do that on-page or your books would be *War and Peace*-style tomes.

Worked Example of a Side Character Arc

Example: Frank from *The Scent of Death*.

Let's use one of my characters as an example. You met Frank earlier—he's from the book I'm currently working on, *The Scent of Death*. If you recall, Frank is gay and in the closet, and struggling to come out to his family and friends. The theme of *The Scent of Death* is all about "saving or to save"—the phrase I've used specifically is: *you can't save everyone because not everyone wants saving.*

Your side character's arc slots into a variation on your theme, it makes your story feel that much more cohesive. Ideally, the bigger the role the side character has, the more relevant their arc should be to the main theme and your hero's arc. You can do this in a couple of ways. The first is to have the side character represent a different take on the theme, in this instance, Frank is saving his identity and mental health rather than saving another person. But I could have Frank represent a positive form of the theme, a negative form of it, or a slide away from the theme and have him staying in the closet, which would result in him ending the book miserable. Another idea I could use is to have a flat character, meaning his relationship with the theme would be unchanging. For example, he could be openly gay at the start of the book and continue to be openly gay at the end.

With Frank, I created him as a variation on the theme. Frank needs to come out in order to save his identity and his mental health.

How does this play out on the page? While Frank has an arc, the resolution of that arc can be shown in a small scene with the protagonist. Frank can come out to his parents with (Mal, the protagonist) there as support or Mal could accidentally out Frank or Mal could be the one pushing Frank through the door to out himself to his family. Either way, Frank's arc is not what the story is about. The story is about Mal and his need to work out that you can't save everyone. Of course, the story *could* be all about Frank's journey—coming out is a huge deal—and that is the plot for some LGBT stories. But that's not what *this* story is about. Frank's coming out forms a small scene and subplot that Mal is involved in. At the same time, it doesn't detract from the main plot line, but supports it by showing another variation on the theme of saving.

Other examples of major character arcs include:

- In *Moana*, Maui learns that he was wrong to steal the Heart of Tefiti and giving it back earns him more love and affection than stealing it ever did.
- Bran Stark in *Game of Thrones* learns to embrace his disability and his new found abilities and use them to take the throne.

Arc it Deeper, Bitch

One effective way of deepening your characterization is to add layers and layers of pressure. The more pressure, the greater the need the character has to change. That's how it works for the hero, but that's also how it works for the side characters.

There's a reason why the faceless "they" say: the greater the sacrifice the bigger the reward. It's because it's true.

The harder the problem, the more pressure it creates. In real life, the more pressure we are under, the less cognitive flexibility we have because all of our brain power is defaulting to solving the problem and relieving the pressure. Which means the less ability we have to mask our behavior. In other words, when we're under intense pressure, we're more likely to show our true selves. This is the case for characters, too; the more pressure you pile onto your side characters and hero, the more they need to default to their most fundamental traits. This pressure forces them (side characters and hero alike) to confront their true selves. As your novel progresses and the pressure increases on the protagonist to grow and change, the pressure should increase on your side characters too. Albeit to a lesser extent, but as a representation of the theme, the plot should have a pressure-inducing load on the side characters too.

For example, with Frank, as the book progresses, his parents could ask about his girlfriend—adding pressure. His parents could ask to meet her—more pressure. His parents could try to integrate her into the family—pressure. There should be slip-ups and close calls in what's said—pressure. Of course, *all* of these scenes may not actually play out on the page, given he's a side character, but some might (with Mal present or as a small part of a scene that's actually focused on Mal) and where they don't happen, on-page conversations can cover what's happened, thus creating the illusion of pressure and change.

STEP 6 PLOT WEAVING SUMMARY

- Where we beat our characters, had sister-lovers, changed, grew and then fell, and arced it deeper, bitch.
- The three main types of arc are: positive, negative, and flat.
- A change arc is most often, although not always, reserved for the protagonist. That's because it's the most dramatic of all arcs and shows a complete transformation and divergence from their personality at the start of the story.
- A growth arc is a little less dramatic, the character is ultimately the same person at their core, but they've grown and developed and perhaps have a different perspective, mindset, learned something new or have a different role in life. Usually, these arcs are found in side characters.
- A fall arc is most often found in villains because it's negative. The character falls away from what's seen as good and moral and ends up in disastrous circumstances. Usually, these characters die, but

they don't have to. Other outcomes can be: corruption, insanity, imprisonment, disillusionment, or anything else devastating you can think of.

- The hero always suffers for the change in their arc, and so should your side characters.
- Let there be consequences for any character's choices. These consequences drive up the tension and create plot points.

Questions to ask yourself when working out who needs an arc:

- Does your character appear three times or less?
- Does your character have sufficient impact on the plot that they change, influence, or sway the protagonist or a storyline?
- Are they one of your main character's best mates, a very key player and therefore appear in the majority of scenes?

All arcs need:

- A character who needs or wants something
- Said character not being able to get that thing
- The character changing or doing something in order to...
- Get the thing!

- Side character arcs can be shown by having a character want something and then showing the outcome of whether or not they get it.
- That said, it can seem flat to the reader if you don't include a reason why they both want that thing and why they get it or not.

You can show changes in character through:

- Voice, tone, and word changes
- Posture and subconscious body language changes
- Mindset shifts
- Action changes

Questions to Think About

1. Thinking about the genre you write in, identify five side characters with arcs.
2. Note down how those side character arcs are portrayed in the stories. Do they have lots of page time? Do you only see the start and conclusion? What can you learn from how they're portrayed?

STEP 7 KILLING YOUR DARLINGS

7.0 KILLING YOUR DARLINGS

Where we sacrifice our darlings, discuss fridges, dick moves of the highest order, Balrogs, and narrowly miss a soap box.

"To make death poignant, make living beautiful. To make us miss characters who will die, make them the very best thing about being alive." Donald Maass, *The Emotional Craft of Fiction*.

There are numerous references to film and movies in this section and because we're talking about death, this section more than any other is rife with spoilers. I mean come on; this chapter is quite literally about creating your own spoilers! Skip this section if you've not read or watched:

Spoiler warning books: *The Fault in Our Stars* by John Green, *The Hate You Give* by Angie Thomas, *A Song of Ice and Fire*, the whole *Game of Thrones* series by George R.R. Martin, *A Christmas Carol* by Charles Dickens, *The Sky Is Everywhere* by Jandy Nelson, *Victor* from the Eden East Series by me!, *Divergent Series* by Veronica Roth, *P.S. I Love You* by Cecelia Ahern,

Point of Origin and *Blow Fly* by Patricia Cornwell, *Our Chemical Hearts* by Krystal Sutherland

Spoiler warning movies: *The Lord of the Rings, Infinity Wars, End Game, Hook, Hercules, Spiderman, The Lion King, The Wolf of Wall Street, The Dark Knight Rises, The Truman Show, Coco*

Spoiler warning TV shows: *Once Upon a Time, Grey's Anatomy, Buffy the Vampire Slayer*

There are two types of writers. The "I spent forever carefully crafting and loving-to-life my darling characters so I couldn't possibly kill them," and the "where's the poison-machete, bitches? Let-me-at-em" type.

Let's take a moment to talk about the skeletal, immortal trickster that's coming for us all: death. No matter your views on death, it's a slippery bastard in fiction. Sometimes writers casually throw out a beheading or three, a cheeky rib-tickling samurai to the gut, or a sly nightshade pill in the protagonist's evening vino-splasho.

But, where's the meaning in those deaths? Where's the elegance? Yes, casual axings and gunshots are sometimes necessary, but we must make sure their impact is at maximum warp. Shakespeare killed 155 characters in his plays, and I can bet you he considered all of their deaths down to the minute detail. No, dear writers, we need to be better than an impromptu offing. What I can tell you about ol' Shakaaaspeare is that he was partial to a knifing[1]. The majority of his deaths were through cheeky stab-stabs. You can get the link to the breakdown of Shakespeare's deaths in the downloadable checklist by visiting: sachablack.co.uk/sidecharacters.

When done correctly, a death can have a monumental impact on your story, characters, and readers alike. It's important to get them right. And given it's a rarer occurrence for your protagonist to die... because then... well there ain't no more story to tell, the large majority of deaths happen to side characters. Let's delve into the murky depths of murder, mayhem, and annihilation, shall we?

Why Do You Need Death in Your Book?

If you write romance, or something where you don't plan on conducting any cut-throat antics, then you might be wondering why on earth you'd need to worry about death? Your characters are going to prance off into the sunset, hand in pudgy hand, singing *the sun will come out, tooomorrow.* But hold up fearless word slingers, all books need some death in them. Story, after all is about change and to create that change, your protagonist needs to experience a form of death in order to improve herself sufficiently so she can defeat the opposing force. And your side characters who have arcs will need a "change" too and "change" really means death.

Types of Death

You might be expecting a slew of dramatic sword-to-artery type descriptions here, but sadly not. I bring you but two types of death. Most writers agree that there are a few types of death. They range from: emotional death, psychological death, philosophical death, occupational death, and the slightly more permanent form... actual fucking death.

I'm sure we could categorize half a dozen other forms of death but I like to keep shit simple. I'm going to describe death in literature as just two variations: actual fucking death (just kidding, let's be professional and go with **tangible death** because I like being matchy-matchy) and **intangible death.**

Intangible Death

This covers all other aspects of death. Less physical, perma-nent death and more figurative death. When we look at story, usually the protagonist doesn't die, although I'm sure we can all name a few instances where that's not the case. The point is, there still needs to be some interaction with death in order for the protagonist to grow enough they can defeat whatever or whoever the villain is.

Let's start with **emotional death**. Romance is an obvious choice here, perhaps the protagonist needs to let go of the ex who gave her crabs before she can really embrace her new love interest. In *P.S. I Love You* by Cecelia Ahern, the protagonist, Holly, needs to learn to move on from the devastating loss from her husband, the acceptance and pushing through grief is the emotion gut punch. This kind of emotional death needs to be significant. It can't be some namby-pamby action that makes your protagonist feel miffed, it has to be so deeply knife-to-the-heart-bruising that it crushes their soul into oblivion. More to the point, it needs to have serious consequences and ramifica-tions. In fact, with all these types of deaths, there should be consequences.

Occupational death is what it says on the tin. Let's say your protagonist is a big banker-wanker, like Jordan Belfort (a real banker and also protagonist of the novel and film *The Wolf of Wall Street)* in order to learn his lesson about defrauding and manipulating the stock market, he lost his status and occupa-tion as an investment banker when he was caught by the FBI. Here endeth his occupation and thus he lives through an occu-pational death. But Jordan is a protagonist. Christof, however, is not. Christof, the director of "The Truman Show" in the movie of the same name, ends up becoming obsolete when Truman uncovers the fact he's in a TV show and demands to leave.

Philosophical, moral, or value-driven death is a type of death that has far-reaching consequences for the protagonist. You'll often see a death like this in a story with a negative story arc or in a villain's redemption arc. A great example of this in a side character is Regina, the Evil Queen from the TV show *Once Upon a Time*. She gives up her evil ways, values, and desires in a bid to become a better person; thus her old philosophy dies in order for her to progress through that growth.

Personality or psychological death is a type of death that impacts who the protagonist or side character is. Now, this one comes with a warning—yes, you can change a character, but remember all we get of the character is what's on the page. If you change them too much, they will no longer feel like the character that started the story. In instances like this, try to only change one aspect, and keep everything else the same. In my third young adult novel, a side character, Kato, goes through a personality death. He loses his brother in book two. He becomes addicted to a particular type of power. This results in a downward spiral and loss of many aspects of his personality, which he will need to overcome if he's going to defeat the enemy with the protagonist. The key with this type of death is that the character has to question who they are, their identity, and where they belong in the world. Trinity, a side character from *The Matrix*, undergoes a value/belief death during the film. The Oracle had previously told her she would fall in love with "The One" but when Neo is convinced he isn't "The One," it shatters Trinity. Thankfully, Trinity rebuilds her belief and her renewed conviction helps Neo find his own self-belief.

Let's move on to tangible death.

Tangible Death

Tangible death is your good ol' eternity in a coffin form of death. Now, much as I'd like to sit here and give you a run-down of different options for how you slay your characters, *makes note for a future book,* that's not what this book is about. Instead, we're going to look at the reasons why you might want to kill a character.

That's really it for this section. Your character actually dies and that's the end of them. You need to ensure there are some consequences in your story and a reaction from your characters, more on this later.

Death Hath No Purpose

The biggest mistake writers make with killing a side character is to do it for no justifiable reason. Something along the lines of "because it seemed like a good idea" or maybe the plot slowed, or you felt like you needed to shake things up again.

No, Darling.

You're not a mixologist. This isn't a bar. We're not shaking up martinis and groping Bond's pe...

Pens..? Pecs?

Anyway, this is your novel. Let your character's death serve a purpose otherwise it's a waste of all the effort your perfectly good braincells put in to create them.

One of my philosophical fears is that when I get to the wrinkled-scrotum stage in my life and look back, none of it means anything. I want to help people, I want to leave the world a little bit better, and bring a smile to people's faces. I want to do something that counts. That way, in my mind, my death will have meaning—or at least, it won't be meaningless.

Death in a story is entirely contextual. One kind of death in one story won't create the same depth of meaning in another story. If you want your character's end to have meaning then connect it to the story. What do I mean by this? Well, if your story theme is revenge then you need to put a spin on any revenge death. Make them have consequences or meaning—for example:

- Protagonist revenge kills henchman A. But then feels no better despite getting revenge [meaning and mindset] and it doesn't help him return his loved one [plot consequence].
- Protagonist revenge kills henchman A. But later finds out that henchman A is his lover's brother. [plot consequence] Thus fucking shit up for his romantic endeavors [meaning].
- Protagonist revenge kills henchman A and realizes that revenge isn't really what he needed after all [meaning] and vows never to kill again. Only he gets put back in the position where he then has to kill the main villain, thereby breaking his vow [plot consequence] and testing his moral fiber.

Each of these three examples provides a deeper meaning or opportunity for the author to explore an emotional depth or philosophical standpoint connected to the theme of revenge, be it: revenge being meaningless or not, every action has a consequence, and whether what we think we want [revenge] is in fact what we need. Each of these deaths would also serve to provide plot complications and conflict.

God, it's fucking glorious, isn't it? Don't you love it when you can be a smart ass and make every element in your book work twice for you?

Alright, we're agreed, you need a "proper good"—this is our new measure—reason to kill off one of your darlings. What, then, are those reasons? And even more important, what are the reasons *not* to?

Let's take a look at other forms of character death that can work as plot devices, pre-plot death, and off-screen deaths.

---

1. https://www.vox.com/2016/1/3/10702004/shakespeare-death-chart

7.1 SEVERAL SHIT REASONS TO KILL CHARACTERS

Look, we all like playing God with our characters. There's nothing better than a little blade tickle to the armpit. But just because you want the stab-candy, doesn't mean you should take it. I can't believe I'm saying this, but sometimes we all need to practice abstinence. Right, let's cover some of the terribly bad reasons why you might want to kill a character off.

Reason 1: It Makes Readers Boo Hoo

I know deep down you're all wanting to cackle at the moon as you wriggle your author fingers and swim in an oceanic-sized pool of your reader's tears. But listen, bitch, making your readers cry *just because* is a dick move of the highest order. Readers won't thank you. They will, however, thank you for a death that makes them sob their heart out because it's full of meaning and connects to the theme and has delightful consequences. If you want to rip your reader's heart out, set up the death, foreshadow that mother like you're Hansel and Gretel in the breadcrumb Olympics.

Look, I don't like being mean okay, and I *really did* LOVE the

Divergent series, truly, I gobbled it up. But Roth got slated for the ending and that's because she betrayed her readers. Tris, the protagonist, was on a heroine's journey; she was building her army and bringing her people together, she was meant to get the guy and save the world. But that's not what happened. Instead, Roth killed Tris off, there was no foreshadowing for that because the foreshadowing hinted at a happily ever after.

Honestly? I think she did it to elicit tears. Sadly, for Roth, that's not the outcome she got. Instead, hordes of fans threw their books across the room as they realized that was a real death they just read. Don't do a Roth. If you're killing a character, drop breadcrumb hints.

Reason 2: For the Shock Factor

Sometimes I wanna throw fireworks onto the bonfire just for shits and giggles. Sometimes I wanna poke my siblings right in the feels, just to see what happens—just for effect. But a really bad time to do something for effect is in a novel. If I've said it once, I'll say it again—everything must serve a purpose, including character deaths.

If you kill a character just to shock your readers because it's unexpected, it's going to feel flat and unfulfilling. I'm paraphrasing the Donald Maass quote from the top of this chapter, but to make a character death meaningful, we should love their life. That means we need time to fall in love with them *before* you off them. Am I saying you can never have a shock death? No, of course not. Arguably, Ned Stark's death in *A Game of Thrones,* was shocking as hell. But for the most part, we need our subconscious to pick up the breadcrumbs of a poignant death, we need time to percolate, to love, to live with them before you authors mercilessly rip them from our mitts and more than any of that, it needs to have a reason.

Reason 3: Privilege, Diversity, and Marginalization

This is a difficult conversation to have. But I'm going to have it anyway, cause it's important, especially in today's society.

One of the worst types of character deaths to write is killing off a marginalized, diverse, or underprivileged character **for no reason.** Now, what I am absolutely not saying is that you can *never* kill off a lesbian or a person of color or other person from a diverse background. Of course, you can. I mean, if you write an epic fantasy book with purely diverse characters, someone's going to die, right? The point is, if you do intend to kill off someone from a marginalized background, you'd better make damn sure that you have a diamond-hard reason for doing it. This killing off of diverse characters (and in particular LGBT+ characters) is common enough—there's a trope named after it, *"Bury Your Gays"*—I'll link to the TV tropes article in the resources section.

There's not enough representation in publishing as it is, I don't want to be ranty, but let's try to keep at least some of the representation in our books alive, shall we?

An example of a character of color dying that's been done well can be found in *The Hate You Give,* by Angie Thomas. Kahil dies early in the book and serves as the catalyst for the entire plot. What's key is that his death is symbolic and serves a purpose. It demonstrates how so many young Black men are wrongly dehumanized into thugs. Starr—the protagonist—spends much of the plot talking about his life, his interests, who he was as a person, which serves to humanize him to the reader and to the "crowds" in the story, preventing them from accepting the police and media's demonized concept of Kahil.

Reason 4: Fridging

If you've never come across the term "fridging," it was

coined after a comic—*The Green Lantern*—where the writers killed off the Green Lantern's partner (Alexandra DeWitt) and stuffed her into a refrigerator.

Why is this bad?

The only reason for her death was to make the Green Lantern hate Major Force more than he already did. Her death didn't solve a problem, it didn't twist the plot, its sole consequence was to heighten one man's hate for another man. I'm trying desperately hard not to jump on a soap box here and stick to story. But come on chaps, can't we do better than that? Killing off women just to further a male character arc is weak at best. Am I saying you can't kill off a male character's love interest? No. Obviously not. There are no rules remember. What I'm saying is that you should have a better reason than "just to serve a male protagonist's character arc." Now, all's fair in gender, and men can be fridged just as much as women. Don't think just because it's two women in love or a more diverse set of characters that it doesn't count as fridging—if anything, it makes it worse because now, you're fridging not just a woman but a marginalized character too. I don't mind confessing that it kills me to say this because I loved this show. But, in *Buffy the Vampire Slayer*, Tara—Willow's girlfriend—is shot. Her death is completely meaningless. She's not fighting to save her friends, she's not on a mission trying to do something. The bullet wasn't even meant for her. Her death was literally meaningless. If your characters are committing themselves to a quest or a purpose and then they die, that's one thing. But a stray bullet killing a character just so that Willow can go nuclear is undoubtably fridging. Likewise, a gender flipped fridge was bestowed upon us by the great George R.R. Martin, who killed off Khal Drogo for the sole purpose of motivating Daenerys in *A Song of Ice and Fire*. Simply, then, fridging refers to killing off a love interest for the sole purpose of motivating a character.

Reason 5: They're Not Staying Dead

If you're writing in a contemporary world without magic, think before killing off a character. In the *Kay Scarpetta* series by Patricia Cornwell, Kay's partner, Benton Wesley, dies in *Point of Origin*. Three books later in *Blow Fly* he reappears. I remember being furious that he'd come back. It made his original death meaningless. Though, I grant that at least two other side characters—Pete and Lucy—who are very close to Kay are in on covering up Benton's death and therefore his "fake" death serves a double purpose of fucking up their lives too.

But the point is, if you're going to bring back a character, you need to make sure there are solid reasons and consequences after both their original death and upon their return. Shit can't just go back to daisies and roses. That's not how real life works.

If you write in a fantasy world, you have the added complication of needing to make sure that any death you create doesn't fuck with the laws of magic you've already established —I learned this lesson the hard way and have spent two years trying to write myself out of a corner.

Alright, enough bitching about the bad reasons, what about the good reasons to kill off a character?

7.2 SEVERAL GOOD REASONS TO KILL A CHARACTER

Enough of the sensible stuff. I think we've had more than enough of all the reasons why you should put the guns away. How about the reasons you *should* get stab-happy?

Reason 1: Firework up the Butt aka Motivation

Right, now I know I just said you should try to avoid the awkward turtle that is fridging, but killing characters does tend to motivate a protagonist. How do you do it without stuffing limbs into fridges?

At the end of the movie *Infinity Wars*, a number of the Avengers die. While this is the physical end of that film, it serves as a longtail catalyst for the remaining Avengers to save them in the next film. I say longtail because there is a five-year time gap between the remaining Avengers realizing they have the power to do something. There is a second death in the final movie *End Game* that serves the motivational purpose better. Black Widow sacrifices herself in order for the Avengers to gain the soul stone. Her death, unlike the deaths of the other characters at the end of *Infinity Wars* is irreversible; they can't bring her back, and therefore it pushes the team to save everyone else to ensure her death wasn't in vain.

In *The Lord of The Rings,* Gandalf confronts the Balrog on the Bridge of Moria and realizes their quest is in danger. He sacrifices himself to save the others, thereby providing motivation for Frodo and the others to march on. Some might argue this isn't a real death motivation because Gandalf comes back to life. However, Frodo and gang don't know he's going to come back to life. Therefore, in their eyes, his death is real and permanent and that's why it's a motivator.

Reason 2: The Dark Night

In every story, there's a moment of darkness for the protagonist. It's also called the "all is lost" moment. It's when the protagonist has lost a "battle" or encounter with the villain or opposing force and they believe the fight is unwinnable. It usually occurs right before they discover the missing puzzle piece or how to change themselves. You usually find it just before the climax of your story begins, and indeed, a character death can force your protagonist into the dark night. Perhaps the loss of a friend or ally or mentor at this point will make them feel like all is lost. A good example of this kind of death is Tiny Tim in *A Christmas Carol.* When the ghost of Christmas yet to come visits Scrooge, he's shown how his actions will lead to Tiny Tim's death. This propels him into and subsequently out of his dark night/all is lost moment.

Reason 3: Realistic

Are your characters in the midst of a massive battle? Are there explosions and sword clashes in your story? Are your character's friends assassins and bad asses? Well then, it's mighty realistic to expect at least one character to die. You'll probably do yourself more of a disservice by not killing a character under these circumstances than by swiftly offing them.

The *Game of Thrones* series is a good example of this. Yes, Martin is excessively stabby, but equally, if no one died there would be some very arched reader eyebrows.

Reason 4: Augments the Theme

The Fault in Our Stars by John Green is about two teenagers, Hazel and Augustus. Both young and therefore shouldn't be experiencing as much death as they are. But the main theme in the book—life and death—requires that there is at least some death in the book. Therefore, when Augustus dies, not only does it rip the reader's heart out, but it is a fulfilling death because it was an expected outcome. The reader knows the book is about life and death, the kids are sick, the breadcrumbs were there, which is why his death serves a purpose and demonstrates the death aspect of the theme.

Reason 5: It Advances the Plot

If a death is necessary to advance the plot, then it's a jolly good idea to fulfill that character death. Indeed, in the example of the Avengers, several of the characters had to die in order to push the remaining Avengers on. Likewise with Dumbledore. And in that train of thought, if a death is foreshadowed, be it for the completion of an arc, because it's right for the plot, because someone needed revenge or otherwise, then that would be rather handy for that death to occur, don't you think? It doesn't mean the consequences of that death have to go to plan though...!

Reason 6: Character Arc Completion

In the movie *Hook*, Rufio, the temporary leader of the Lost Boys dies. But his death is both meaningful and purposeful. In a way, his death completes his character arc. When Peter returns to Neverland there's tension and angst between him and Rufio. Rufio despises Peter. But as it turns out, the only reason Rufio is behaving like this is because he actually looks up to Peter and just wanted to be like him. For him to lay down his life to protect Peter makes total sense. It completes Rufio's arc and the consequence is that Peter is even more motivated to defeat Captain Hook.

In the same way, Tony Stark from the Avengers movies had to die to complete his character arc. Of course, I acknowledge he was a protagonist in his own movies but he was less so in the final movies where they were all protagonists or perhaps all supporting characters. Tony started out as a very selfish, self-absorbed character only concerned with his own interests. By the end of the movies, he's selfless to the point of sacrificing himself to save the rest of the world. What a 180-degree turn!

7.3 PRE-PLOT DEATH

There are two cheeky types of character death that are often not utilized by authors: pre-plot and off-screen deaths. Now the obvious reason is because the reader doesn't get to "see" the death. But hold your horses, sunshine, these can both be useful techniques. Let's discuss...

Pre-Plot Death

A pre-plot death happens before the "present" time in the book you're reading (or writing). For example, in *The Sky Is Everywhere* by Jandy Nelson, Bailey—the protagonist's sister—dies before the story begins. It opens with Lennie, the protagonist, reeling from Bailey's death and trying to learn how to live again without her sister. Another story that follows a similar plot device is *Our Chemical Hearts* by Krystal Sutherland, where Henry, the protagonist, falls for Grace, the love interest. But prior to the story starting, Grace loses her boyfriend. This creates conflict and barriers preventing Grace and Henry from getting together, even though Grace's ex is dead.

Pre-plot side character deaths are usually there to haunt the protagonist or in Grace's case haunt a side character. The death, though, should create problems for the characters in real time in the story. This means the death or the consequences should come up repeatedly, especially if the character that died was significant to the protagonist or is significant to someone who is significant to the protagonist—as in Henry and Grace's case. Another example of this kind of death serving a purpose in the "present" of a story is Lyanna Stark in *Game of Thrones*. Lyanna was Ned Stark's sister and mother of Jon Snow, something Ned had to keep secret, which caused untold conflict in the series.

If you choose to create a pre-plot death, it should—like the other forms of death—serve a purpose, create conflict, issues, or haunt a character in the present story. Try to loop the death in at multiple points or have it affect multiple characters. If you don't have these repeated touch points, the death loses its significance and just becomes another piece of backstory. If you want a pre-plot death to be meaningful and play a role in the present story, you need these touch points.

One other thing to note is that too often pre-plot deaths are from characters who are nothing but cute, super femme, perfectly perfect, and delightful humans with no flaws. Obviously, your character is going to be haunted by the loss of this person, because they were perfectly perfect and created solely for your character to miss. Bitch please. Let's sharpen the realism blades and make the characters flawed and, in those flaws, find things for your character to miss. It will make the dead character less of a clichéd plot device and more of a realistic loss for the protagonist or other characters.

Off-screen Deaths

Off-screen deaths happen before or during the story, the important thing is that the moment of death doesn't appear on the page. In other words, the reader (and the protagonist) do not see the stab-stab action or the hollow crackle of a dying breath. That can, however, see a retelling of that death. If, say, a side character was at the death they might convey what happened.

There are a number of cautions here. Readers want to see action. They come to your stories for the good bits, the juicy squelch of a knife gliding through innards. They want to see and feel the heart wrench as a favorite character cops it and dances into the unknown. Take that away and you risk pissing off your readers. But equally, in giant battles, dozens of characters are going to die, and does every bit part and cameo deserve a three-page eulogy describing the intimate details of their denouement? No, they do not. The general rule of thumb here is that the bigger the character the bigger the death scene needs to be. Small bit part character? Well, the chances of anyone crying over their off-screen death are small. Big side character? I urge you not to behead them off-screen.

An example of an off-screen death includes Tonks, Moody, and Lupin from the final *Harry Potter* book, all of whom die off-screen during the final battle. In the Pixar film *Coco*, Mamá Coco, Miguel's great-grandma passes away at the end of the film—we don't see her death, just her photo placed with the photos of Miguel's other ancestors.

Additional Marketing Material

Let us pause the craft chat for a brief moment. As discussed, unless there's a reason for writing them into the story, these are deaths the reader doesn't get to "see" on the page. But you as the author know what happened, you know how these deaths played out. Why not use that knowledge to write the scenes and then parcel them up as reader magnets and giveaways to encourage readers onto your mailing list... *which you should have by the way, but that's another conversation for another book.*

7.4 DEATH AND SIDE CHARACTERS

There is a sliding scale to this death business—some deaths resonate deep enough that we weep for days over bent spines and coffee-stained pages. Some character deaths leave us with a hangover and an urge to get cannon-happy with the author. But how do we create those feelings in readers, and does it matter which side characters die?

Yes, and also no.

The bigger the character, the more important and mean-ingful their death should be. Here are some questions to ask yourself when determining how meaningful a character death is:

- Are they close to the protagonist? Does the protagonist care deeply about the character?
- Are they a major side character?
- Do they represent the theme?
- Are they involved in multiple plots?

If the answer to any of those questions is yes then the

chances are you need to do more with their death than a throw-away axe and one-liner "she died" explanation.

Cameo Deaths

Much as writing a six-page epic battle to the death for every character would be fun, someone has to be the sacrificial lamb that gets nothing but a flick of a switch blade to the carotid and a three-word ending. Cameos are it. These guys don't need an emotional outpouring to make their death meaningful. In fact, you don't need to make their death meaningful at all. Ultimately, *they* aren't meaningful to the plot. Freely slaughter your cameos and end their plot participation with a brief one-line obituary if you care to.

Minor Character Deaths

Minor characters' deaths are a little trickier than cameos, but only just. I suppose the real question is how minor is the character?

If a character only appears once or twice then axe them and think nothing of it. If they're your protagonist's favorite bar tender, then while you don't need a three-hour eulogy, they're going to feel a little bit sad, unless your protagonist is a cold-hearted fish. Your reader needs to experience those sad-feels. Show 'em. And I do mean *show* and not *tell*. Just don't spend four paragraphs showing, a nod to the moment and the feels is all you need.

Major Characters

Here is where you need to throw the bulk of your meaningful death weight. Logically you can't off a major character without allowing at least some page time to show the death happening or the consequences of that loss.

Some points to note: as an author you're well within your rights to off any character you like. But be warned, when you off a major character there are always risks of reader backlash; make sure you're killing them for the right reason—if in doubt, re-read 7.2.

Ned Stark, from the *Game of Thrones* series was a controversial offing, because it was unexpected. But because Mr. Martin did it well enough, it fueled (for the most part) reader enthusiasm rather than detracting from the story.

In TV shows, the last side character to make me bawl like a baby was McDreamy, aka Dr. Derek Shepherd from *Grey's Anatomy*, and one more example, Buffy's mom, Joyce Summers, from *Buffy the Vampire Slayer*.

Each of these characters meant something to the protagonist. Derek was Meredith's soul mate or "person." He was the father of her children and her best friend. Joyce was Buffy's mom. Each of the characters who died left a mark on both the protagonist and the story that lasted long after their death. Half a dozen seasons on and Derek is still having an impact on Meredith. These major side characters should be involved in subplots, in conflict and in emotional scenes and have a swathe of details attached to them. Then their post-death impact lasts.

Derek, for example, married Meredith on a Post-it, which they promptly hung over their bed and was over her bed for years after he died.

Hear ye, hear ye, there's two key things you need to know if you're planning to kill off a major character:

1. There's an emotional reaction from your protagonist and other side characters
2. There's a consequence, be it emotional, motivational, plot or otherwise

Let's dive into a bit more detail.

Oh, but before I forget, you can get the side characters checklist to help you kill your darlings by visiting: sachablack. co.uk/sidecharacters

7.5 EMOTIONAL REACTIONS TO DEATH

Death is a big thing. It tears someone meaningful in our lives away from us. Forever. Don't underestimate the power of that experience for your characters—and consequently your readers. We've talked about needing to create meaningful deaths for your major side characters, but how? That's what we're going to look at now.

"Creating pain in death isn't really about losing the person. Of course, that's horrendous and awful. We all know that pain. But what truly conveys the significance of loss to a reader is the intangible thing a hero can't touch..." Sacha Black, *The Anatomy of Prose*.

Death—or being parted from loved ones—is terrible. Everyone knows that pain. But what truly makes us relate to the character's pain is the universal elements. It's a misnomer that to create big universal feelings you have to describe giant emotions. It's actually the small, unique, and intangible things about our loved ones that create that effect. In fact, the more unique to us and our relationships, the more universal it is and the emotion you evoke. Sounds like a paradox, right? It kinda is. Stick with it.

To create meaning in a character death, allow your living characters to miss the quirks, the memories and the little things the dead character did. Here's a little snippet of flash fiction I wrote a while back when trying to capture what I meant by this exact concept.

"It wasn't the car, the house or the ring. It was the way her hand touched mine as we drifted to sleep. How her skin tasted like forest flowers, and mornings always smelt like fresh brewed coffee. Yeah, that's what I fell in love with." Sacha Black.

It's those details that a reader can relate to. What hurts is

> "...the ache of knowing that settles when you realize you'll never make another memory and the edges of this one are already fading." Sacha Black, *The Anatomy of Prose*.

To make a death meaningful, the reader has to see that character living life and loving, caring and having a meaningful relationship with the protagonist and other side characters. Make sure you have details and nuances that are meaningful only to that character and the protagonist. Give your living characters something to miss about the character who is dying.

Death Details

Next time you're stuck trying to make a character death meaningful, brainstorm what loss feels like to you. Note down some significant memories you have with someone who has passed. What details can you draw on from those memories? Here are some examples of details to help you:

- Smells you associate with them
- A habit or quirk they had
- A location you used to visit together
- A specific holiday you went on

- An item of clothing or jewelry they always wore
- Another person who was important to them (and why)
- An object, antique or item they loved
- A flower or decoration they loved
- A particular food or drink they always ate / drank
- An in-joke, phrase, or relationship language that you shared

Death and Senses

If you want to create emotion in readers, the quickest way to elicit it is through engaging the senses in your writing. Our brains are amazing little critters, regardless of whether we perform an action or whether we *think* about performing that action, the same area in our brain lights up. This means, even if we're only *thinking* of the smell of roses, the same area of your brain that processes the *actual* smell of a rose when it's wafted under your nose is activated. This means you can create emotional reactions in your readers by engaging their senses.

But Sacha, how the hell do you use the senses with your character deaths? I mean, no one wants to sniff rotten flesh and bloated corpse gas do they... too graphic? Anyway...

Consider the relationship your protagonist has with the character that's passed away. Is there a particular sense that the dead character made your protagonist tap into? For example, did the dead character always wear the same perfume?

When Trey (my protagonist's love interest) dies at the end of *Victor* the second book in the series, Eden misses how he always smelled of frankincense and summer nights. She hunts for anything that smells of him but can never quite get the scent of him right. It's a constant reminder of the loss and therefore a constant emotional prod for the reader.

You don't have to stick with smell though, if a character

used to hunt, perhaps it's the sound of rifle barrels opening and closing, or the click-snap of a trigger that affects the still-living characters. Perhaps it was touch and the way the dead character used to rub his thumb, or maybe the way he stroked the palm of the protagonist's hand.

Don't forget you can learn more about using the senses in your prose, in my writing craft course dedicated to the topic. It's over three hours of content with multiple bonus videos; find out more at sachablack.co.uk/senses.

7.6 DEATH'S CONSEQUENCE

Just as you must have a meaning for the death you're writing, there must also be a consequence. Can you imagine if people collapsed in the middle of the street flopping and fidgeting until they laid inhumanly still and no one did or said a goddamn thing? You'd think there was an outbreak of neighborly psychopathy. That's what happens when there aren't any consequences to a death in your novel. But what are the three most common forms of consequence? Plot, conflict, and emotion. Let's take them in turn.

Plot Consequence

Plot consequences occur when the death has a direct impact on an aspect of the plot or a subplot. For example, if the only magician with the knowledge of how to enter a particular realm—one your protagonist really needs to go to—spontaneously drops dead, well that's going to cause a problem for your protagonist, isn't it?

The most important question is how does the loss of this character affect your protagonist's and side character's goals?

Does the death create conflict or obstacles? Does it leave a hole in your protagonist's heart? Maybe your protagonist's team is a man down and needs to readjust. Too often in novels there's no consequence after the death of a major character and that's what makes it meaningless.

When Uncle Ben dies in *Spiderman*, it rocks Peter's world. He spirals and then becomes highly motivated to do something about it. The consequence is twofold here: first sadness (the emotion) then action. Ben's death may have been sad, but it drives the plot forward.

Mufasa's death in *The Lion King* has a consequence. It pushes the plot on because Simba—Mufasa's son—leaves the pride. This is the catalyst for Simba to grow and develop enough so he can complete his character arc and defeat his father's murderer.

You can always subvert expectations and indeed when you do, it often creates excellent plot twists. Which is why the lack of death can create plot problems. If, for example, your protagonist is a highly trained assassin who kills for a living, then there's unlikely to be any emotional consequences to them ending lives. But what if they're at the end of a long arc of realizing they want to quit the killing game? While "assassinating people" wouldn't create plot consequences, there could easily be occupational (plot) consequences for killing (or not as the case may be) another character. And what if that side character left alive then decides to cause chaos for the hero?

However you decide to create consequences in the plot, the vast majority of the time, the consequence should form a new obstacle for the protagonist and crew to get over.

Conflict Consequence

An easy one to understand, if for example your protagonist's love interest gets offed, then they're going to be pretty pissed, and it will heighten the level of conflict between protagonist and villain—though do watch for instances of fridging.

It doesn't have to be a love interest though—if a villain kills any character that means something to the hero it's going to create conflict. And of course, if the protagonist kills a character, then this can create conflict too.

In *The Dark Knight Rises*, Batman has to make a choice between saving Harvey Dent and Rachel Dawes. Harvey and Rachel are engaged although Batman loves Rachel too. Batman thinks he's saving Rachel, but the Joker tricked him and he ends up saving Harvey which creates huge conflict between Harvey and Batman because Harvey wanted Batman to save Rachel too.

Consider:

- How does the death make the protagonist and side characters feel?
- Do any of the characters resent each other or have negative emotions towards each other as a result of the death?
- Who is to blame or who do the characters think is to blame?
- Has the death meant the loss of key information or created misinformation or misunderstandings?

Emotional Consequences

If your average hero kills a person, there's likely to be an emotional consequence. Taking life is serious and something that stays with a person forever. But regardless of whether your character has killed someone or whether the character died of other causes, there should be an emotional response.

We all know how we personally react to death, whether you're a hardened stoic or a wailer isn't relevant. You need to ask yourself, what would be in character for them? How do their traits affect their emotional well-being? And their reactions to emotionally taxing events?

Just like all humans, every character should have a baseline of emotions. Think of one of your loved ones, be it a friend or family member. Hold them in your mind and try to picture a number of interactions with them. I bet you can choose a single descriptive emotional word to describe them. Perhaps they're happy and perky 80% of the time, or perhaps they're more brooding and sullen. Whatever their normal baseline emotion, it's when they diverge from that emotional point that you know something is up. If your sullen moody friend suddenly starts behaving perky then you're going to raise an eyebrow, either something really amazing just happened or they're masking their true feelings.

You need to look at your side characters with the same critical eye. Highly emotional events will force a character to move away from their baseline emotion. But that doesn't mean you have to go the predictable route either. For example, if your protagonist is stoic normally, would the death of a loved one make them *more* stoic and withdrawn or would it have the opposite effect and make them grieve in a much more emotionally overt way? Either way, they wouldn't stay at the same level of stoicism after a loved one died.

STEP 7 KILLING YOUR DARLINGS
SUMMARY

- Where we sacrificed our darlings, discussed fridges, dick moves of the highest order, Balrogs, and narrowly missed a soap box.
- There are two types of character death: tangible and intangible.
- Tangible death is the stabby, poisoned, permanent type of physical death.
- Intangible death covers all other aspects of death. Less physical, permanent death and more figurative death. This type of death includes emotional, occupational, philosophical, and psychological.
- Emotional death happens when the protagonist has their heart ripped out—most commonly found in romance novels. Occupational death happens when a character loses their vocation and it rocks their world. Philosophical death happens when a character has a moral, or value-based death; for example, a character deciding to stop being a "player" and becoming a monogamist. Or a villain undergoing a redemption arc. Psychological death is

a type of death that impacts who the protagonist is. Now this one comes with a warning: yes, you can change a character, but remember all we get of the protagonist is what's on the page. If you change them too much, they will no longer feel like the protagonist that started the story. In instances like this, try to only change one aspect, and keep everything else the same.

Reasons not to kill characters:

- It makes readers cry
- Just for effect or shock value
- They're a diverse character and there's no other justifiable reason for doing it
- They're not staying dead
- You're fridging a character

Good reasons for killing a character:

- To motivate a character. Killing characters does tend to motivate a protagonist, but don't fridge them!
- To throw a protagonist into the dark night
- Because it's a realistic plot point
- It augments the theme
- It advances the plot
- Completes a character arc

- A pre-plot death happens before the "present" time in the book you're reading. Pre-plot side character deaths are usually there to haunt the protagonist or another character or create problems for them. This means the death, or the consequences of it, tend to come up over and over again during the story, especially if the character that died was significant to the protagonist.

- An off-screen death happens off the page. In other words, the reader (and the protagonist) does not see the stab-stab action or the hollow crackle of a dying breath. There are a number of cautions here. Readers want to see action. But equally, in giant battles, dozens of characters are going to die, and does every bit part and cameo deserve a three-page eulogy describing the intimate details of their denouement? No, they don't.

If you kill a supporting character, you need to ensure there are two things shortly thereafter:

1. An emotional reaction from your protagonist and other side characters
2. A consequence, be it emotional, plot, motivational, or otherwise

- Death—or being parted from loved ones—is awful. But what truly makes us relate to the character's pain are the universal elements. The intangible things about our loved ones that were both unique to them and unique to our relationship with them. That includes character quirks and memories of the little things they did.

If you want your character's end to have meaning then connect it to the story. If your story theme is revenge then you need to put a spin on any revenge death. Make them have consequences or meaning. Details help to create meaning too. Here are some examples of details to help you:

- Smells you associate with the lost character
- A habit or quirk they had
- A location you used to visit together
- A specific holiday you went on
- An item of clothing or jewelry they always wore
- Another person who was important to them (and why)
- An object, antique or item they loved
- A flower or decoration they loved
- A particular food or drink they always ate / drank
- An in-joke, phrase, or relationship language that you shared

For conflict creation consider how the emotional responses can create conflict; for example, answer the following:

- How does the death make the protagonist and side characters feel?
- Do any of the characters resent each other or have negative emotions towards each other as a result of the death?
- Who is to blame or who do the characters think is to blame?
- Has the death meant the loss of key information or created misinformation or misunderstandings?

Questions to Think About

1. What character death had the most significant impact on you?
2. Brainstorm a list of character deaths from your genre. What can you learn from how they're written?

STEP 8 FIGHT TO THE DEATH

8.0 FIGHT TO THE DEATH

Where we eat jelly and trifle, discover books have orgasms, discuss big O's, fight, fight, fight, and realize I'm a bit more sordid than is polite.

Spoiler warnings for books: *The Hunger Games* by Suzanne Collins, *The Chronicles of Narnia* by C.S. Lewis, *Bridget Jones's Diary* by Helen Fielding, *Six of Crows* by Leigh Bardugo

Spoiler warnings for movies: *Mean Girls, Toy Story, G.I. Jane*

Spoiler warnings for TV shows: *Prison Break, Sex Education*

Every book I've written on characters has a chapter on conflict. Why? Because conflict is the source of change. It's the driving force bubbling between the lines of blood splattered ink. Conflict is that sweet jelly and trifle pudding that we lap up after a juicy meal.

Creating conflict is as simple as **A** + **B** = **C**. Or in literary terms: **The existence of a goal + prevention of the goal being achieved = conflict.**

Create a goal... Stop the goal coming to fruition. Usually, we think of goals in terms of the hero because the hero's goal is driving the plot. But we're here to focus on the side characters. Which means you need to know:

1. What is your side character's goal?
2. What are you going to do to stop her from getting it?

There are three main types of conflict which I explained in my book *10 Steps to Hero:*

"**Macro conflict** - These are large scale world wars, society against the hero, often found in dystopian novels as the 'final' villain that needs defeating. But this could be any war that spans more than just the hero. It could cross states, history, natural forces, the law, races and more. For example, the faction system that categorizes every citizen in the *Divergent* series by Veronica Roth, or the man-killing Triffid plants in *The Day of The Triffids* by John Wyndham.

Micro conflict - This is a more interpersonal form of conflict — the battles the hero has with personal relationships, for example, between lovers, friends, family, colleagues, and enemies. In *Me Before You* by Jojo Moyes, the entire plot is based on a micro conflict. Will has a motorcycle accident that leaves him with a desire to end his life. Until Lou rolls into his world and tries to change his mind. Their desires—Lou's love for him, and his desire to die—smash into each other as they are in direct opposition.

Inner conflict - This is the smallest unit of conflict as it's internal only to the hero. It's the conflict the hero has with his own flaws, emotions and values. While it's the most isolated conflict, it's usually the most heart-wrenching as it's the conflict closest to the reader — particularly if you write in closer points of view like first person or third person limited.

Game of Thrones by George R.R. Martin is rife with inner conflict. One of Martin's specialties is giving characters conflicting values and loyalties. Jamie Lannister (known as the Kingslayer) killed the very king he swore to protect."

Conflict by Side Character Type

Let's look at the types of side character and their involvement with conflict. First in then, we have the cameo.

Cameos are the tiniest of characters, appearing for mere fleeting beats in a story. Logically then, they should have the least impact on conflict, if any.

Minor characters are still in a class of lesser importance but because they frequent the page more often, there is at least the occasional opportunity for them to impact the conflict. This, though, may be less about them as characters and more about the information they bring or an action they take, like refusing to give the protagonist a name, or telling a henchman of their uninvited presence etc.

Major characters then, can wade hand and foot into the action. They should smother themselves in it like latex and lube, while pouting and singing hey sugar come and... Wait. Wrong book.

Major side characters can and should be direct causes of problems for the protagonist. A major character's actions, opinions, and conversations should meddle with or create conflict and tension on a significant level for the protagonist. They're far more likely than the other side characters to be physically involved and present in any conflict scenes.

One additional point here, if I may. Where possible, any reign of delicious torment and terror a side character brings on the protagonist should be as a result of them trying to achieve their own goals.

Balancing Conflict

If you don't layer your conflict, and you only have world ending levels of conflict at every opportunity, it's like electrocuting your readers over and over again. They need the pace to be varied. Too much conflict and tension keeps them sprinting instead of allowing for recovery. This is where your side characters come in.

Macro-conflict will always involve your protagonist, in *The Hunger Games* the macro conflict is between Katniss and The Capitol. But the side characters slide in to give a dose of micro and inner conflict on the side. For example, Katniss has to physically battle the other tribute side characters in the games. She has to battle her own tingly nether regions because she has vagina-lust for both Peeta and Gale—hello, untold inner conflict.

You can use your side characters then to balance out the conflict, introduce narrower, more interpersonal forms to vary the emotional tension and pace.

The Impossible Choice

A quick note on the impossible choice. One of the most acute forms of conflict for a character is the impossible choice. A choice that, when faced, is impossible to decide upon. Examples include a gay character with disapproving parents—tell their parents and risk being disowned, or stay in the closet and risk losing the love of your life. There's no good choice here, no answer that's going to keep everyone happy. Thus, it is an impossible choice. These choices are powerful for a reader because placed in the same position, a reader wouldn't be able to make a good choice either. You literally create tension because the reader can't predict which bad choice the protagonist will make or what the outcome of that decision will be.

You should have at least one impossible choice in your story. *Should* being that wonderful word filled with expectation and pressure. There are no rules. But remember, in story structure, the protagonist will face a question or huge obstacle at the climax of the story, the harder the choice, the more impossible it seems, the harder your reader will grip the page. However, just because big-bad-protagonist-bollocks takes center stage and gets an impossible choice isn't to say your side characters can't have them too. In *Sex Education,* the Netflix show, Eric Effiong is Otis's best friend—therefore a major side character. He's Nigerian/Ghanaian and gay and his family is religious, leading him to face the impossible choice I mentioned above.

Time as a Pressure

Just a short note to highlight the fact that if you can add a time pressure to your story, it raises the stakes. Instead of just needing to get to the gem, trying to get to the gem before the volcano blows up makes the action that much more intense.

Maslow's Hierarchy of Needs

Maslow's Hierarchy of Needs warrants a brief segue as it's rife with the potential for creating conflict.

Maslow was a psychologist, and famed for having created the Hierarchy of Needs theory in 1954. It lays out all the needs of a human. It starts with basic needs like food, water, and shelter. Then progresses to security and safety, then belonging and love, esteem, and last, self-actualization.

Of course, you can create conflict using the higher needs too, although the higher you go, the more personal the conflict is likely to be. Self-actualization is an internal battle to achieve your personal potential. It is influenced less by external factors and more by personal grit and determination. Self-actualization is in the name: it only affects the "self," whereas basic needs like food and water are a global need and affect billions.

How does it work to create conflict? Well, the more basic the need, the more generic the conflict. Everyone needs food and water or we die, right? The higher the need goes though, the more internal the conflict becomes. With self-actualization, no two people's self-actualization is going to look the same. One character might want to win entrance to a prestigious folk singing academy. Another might want to float their business on the stock market, another character might want their pet frog to win the frog Olympics.

8.1 INNER CONFLICT

You can't allow all of your side characters from cameos through to major side characters to have inner conflicts. There simply isn't the space, there's only one Leo Tolstoy. Your protagonist will face the biggest inner conflict during your story, which means the only other characters that should experience any kind of conflict should be major side characters. But their inner turmoil won't be displayed in the same level of depth as your protagonist. Let's look at what this means.

Wounds

Wounds are the most likely source of any inner conflict. A wound is an event in the past that caused damage to your character. For example, losing a loved one, being responsible for a death, going to war. Something that is traumatic enough it marks their personality and creates a flaw that prevents them from achieving their "best."

Wounds are a fantastic source of inner conflict because they generate such powerful flaws. For example, in the book I'm currently writing, *The Scent of Death,* Mal is present when his big brother dies and blames himself for not being able to save him. This leads him to think he has to save everyone he loves, which is why he's over-protective and tries to save everyone—even those that don't want to be saved. But for Frank, Mal's best friend, he's afraid to come out because his parents have expressed homophobia in the past—creating a fear wound.

One of the most important factors of including a wound is that the wound actually impacts the current plot. It's pointless creating a wound unless it's going to do something. That goes for your side characters too.

Do your side characters need wounds? That depends. Are they going to have an arc? If they are, then yes, yes, they do need to have a wound—that wound will create the obstacle they need to overcome in order to complete their arc.

False Beliefs

Lying is bad, it always gets you into trouble... if you're found out that is. Though sadly, most of us are. And yet, we continue to do it anyway, and especially to ourselves. You may have heard of the "lie your character believes," and if you haven't then buckle up.

One of the most important consequences to your side character's wound is that it should have created a false belief or lie they believe that is hampering them from completing their character arc.

For example, Mal believes he should save everyone he loves. But it's causing problems for him because not everyone should be saved and more importantly not everyone *wants* to be saved. Frank experienced his parents making homophobic comments, which is why he believes he can't come out to his family. But instead of assuming his family would accept him and love him, he builds up a myth and assumption. This lie holds him back and prevents him from having proper relationships and connections with partners.

The lie is your side character's darkness—uncovering the lie for what it is will push them into the light.

And of course, the lies can be generated by other side characters too.

> **Example:** In *Bridget Jones's Diary* by Helen Fielding, Bridget's love interest is Mark Darcy. However, she can't be with him because she believes the lie that another character, Daniel Cleaver, told her—she believes that Mark is a liar and a cheater and Bridget doesn't want to date a cheater. Thus, Daniel as a side character has both created conflict and the lie Bridget believes.

Representing the Wound Tangibly

Every wound has a consequence for the character because it generates a flaw which then prevents them from achieving their goal. However, that's surface level and wholly obvious. My question to you is, can you do more with it? Can you make it work twice for you or connect it to other aspects of your story?

While it's not always possible, if you have your protagonist and side characters present together when past wounds are created, this is one way to harness the wound. Side characters can use their knowledge to stir the proverbial pot in present time. Perhaps the characters disagree about what happened. Maybe the side character thinks it was the protagonist's fault, maybe his siblings think he should have handled things differently. Or perhaps the side character harbors a fear because they blame themselves and that's why they can't connect with the protagonist. Having a side character who wasn't present when your protagonist's wound was created can cause all sorts of conflict. For example, what if there's a communication issue

and the side character just can't understand how your protagonist feels? What if the protagonist experienced the event with
side character A and developed a really close relationship with
them and that causes problems for side character B who's
falling in love with the protagonist?

Perhaps one of the side characters caused or created the
wound. How does that impact their relationship?

But what if characters don't meet until the wound is well
established? Take *Six of Crows* by Leigh Bardugo—Kaz wears
gloves constantly, never taking them off until he's forced. There
are dozens of rumors in his local area that follow him around
giving outlandish reasons as to why he wears those gloves. It
even spawned a nickname "Dirtyhands." But really, they're a
symbol of his wound: when he was a boy, his father died, then
his brother contracted a plague-like illness, it killed his brother
and almost killed him, he woke up on a cremation boat
surrounded by bloated skin and dead bodies. Kaz subsequently
hates the feel of flesh and wears gloves to protect his skin. The
wound has a tangible consequence, and it's the same for all of
the characters. The other characters are curious and judgey,
and the gloves get in the way of Kaz and Inej forming a relationship because he can't touch her.

Inej is traumatized from working in a brothel, it leaves a
permanent psychological *and* physical scar (where she had her
"ownership" tattoo removed). This scar causes a problem later
in the book when Inej has to pretend to be from the same
brothel in order to sneak into a prison. She has the tattoo
painted back on but it doesn't look right, which is why she gets
caught—a symbolic gesture indicating she's not over her
wound yet.

In *Toy Story*, Buzz Lightyear represents his wound through
his spacesuit. He keeps his helmet done up at all times; this is a
representation of his commitment to the space rangers and the
fact he can't let go. It doesn't open until his dark night when he

realizes the truth and can let go of the space rangers and begin his life as a toy.

Consequences and Confrontation

Regardless of whether it's your protagonist dealing with conflict or your side characters, the best form of conflict forces a character to confront their flaw. Kaz, in the above section, wants revenge on the man who is responsible for his brother's death. In order to do that, he needs a large sum of money—enter the plot problem. If he breaks a prisoner out of the highest security prison, he earns millions of pounds—enough to seek revenge. But in order to get into the prison he has to take his gloves off, which causes all kinds of anxiety attacks and conflict for him.

See how cleverly you can weave wounds and conflict into consequences and problems?

Types of Inner Conflict

Love

Love is perhaps the easiest plotline to throw ideas out for. Side characters can easily meddle in the protagonist's love affairs. And not just by having affairs with the hero. They could spread secrets and lies, or misinformation, or perhaps just an innocent miscommunication. Or they could date the one person the protagonist loves—a common trope in romance and YA. In *Mean Girls*, Regina George dates the high school jock who Cady Heron—the protagonist—falls for.

And what if the protagonist wants to sleep with the side character because they're wildly attracted to them—but they know they're trouble...? That's the best kind of trouble if you ask me!

Values and Morals

Side characters with differing values are ripe for conflict. A value is something that has worth or importance to the person whose value it is. It's because we hold our values as important that we tend to get a bit haughty about them if someone goes against or breaks one of them. Villains are especially good at that—look at Hannibal Lecter, you don't want to be impolite around him or you're going to be on the dinner menu.

But we can create problems for our side characters when their inner values and morals conflict against each other. For example, what if your side character believed in human rights, but didn't believe in abortion or euthanasia? These two things are polar opposites. Or you could pit your protagonist and side characters against each other—both united in their cause in ensuring human rights, but one character doesn't believe in "all" human rights. Hey presto, have a slab of conflict, thank you very much.

Beliefs

Be they religious or familial can cause stacks of conflict. If your character comes from a conservative family, for example with antiquated beliefs, but they've grown up in a modern more liberal environment, it's going to cause inner conflict between what they want to do and what their family believes they should do.

Other areas that you can use to create inner conflict for your characters include:

Self-image—perhaps more relevant for contemporary stories, romances, or high school stories. Be honest now, how many of us are secretly riddled with myths about how we look? These worries can cause numerous barriers stopping characters opening up or connecting because of fear of judgment. It can lead characters to tell lies or misunderstand comments.

Religion—religion is rife with conflict. It's hard to maintain faith—in anything—and it must be worked at, that in itself is a form of inner conflict. Romance is often in conflict with religion if two characters fall for each other but are from different backgrounds. Questioning one's faith, science versus religion or modern societal values versus more traditional religious values all create conflict.

Politics—I loathe politics, but it's certainly a good way to create inner conflict, pitting a character's political views against their moral views, old inner values against new ones. Don't keep yourself in a box; you don't have to use more commonly known politics like republican versus democrat or conservative versus liberal. You can make up new political systems in your worlds and pit your characters' moral values against societal politics.

Existential—if you make it to old age without having had an existential crisis then share your secrets, oh wise one. Many of us go through periods of existential crisis, it's the ultimate inner conflict. Why are we here? What are we supposed to do? Does any of it even matter? These questions drive personal conflict and are a great way to get a character to make a series of bad decisions based on their crisis.

8.2 MICRO CONFLICT

Micro conflict is a step up and out from inner conflict. And excitingly for this book, it's where side characters really come into their own. Micro conflict is a more interpersonal form of conflict—it's the battles characters have with personal relationships, between lovers, friends, family, colleagues, and enemies etc.

Rather than being inward focused like inner conflict, micro conflict is firmly wedged in the outer world between two characters. For example, in *Harry Potter*, when Hermione and Ron start arguing (because they fancy the pants off each other but can't bring themselves to admit it) it's a form of micro conflict.

To save repeating myself in each conflict section, let me say this: all of the conflict ideas from the previous chapter are relevant here too. Politics? Cool, that can create micro conflict between characters as well as inner conflict. Instead of having the character's politics butt up against their own morals or values, have them conflict with another character's political stance. Micro conflict rather than causing problems inside a single character, requires two or more characters all brushing up against each other in a stroppy, hand flappy, bitch slappy kind of way. The point is, you can use the causes of conflict that have come before. Instead of going over old ground, I'll just fling some ideas around the conflict cauldron.

Consequences

One area that does bear repeating are conflict consequences. Consequences are the absolute do or die, must-not-be-forgotten aspect of conflict. Just like inner conflict, there must be a consequence to any micro conflict that's created.

Consequences, generally speaking, come in two forms: a positive consequence or a negative one. For the first 75% of your novel, the majority of consequences should be negative. This negative consequence will create plot problems and complications which drive the action forward and your protagonist towards the climax of your story.

What do consequences look like?

Pretend you're a parent and you're telling off kiddo. If kiddo shaved the cat and poured honey and hot pink goose feathers dipped in acid on its raw skin*, you're probably going to want a severe consequence. But in order to give that consequence, you need to know what your kid cares about. There's no point telling him he can't go to the park for a month if he'd rather be playing on his Nintendo Switch. No, a far more reliable and useful punishment would be to put his Switch in a bucket of bleach and hope the fucking thing melts into oblivion.

What I'm trying to say is, your conflict consequences need to mean something to the characters. What do they care about? Consequence that. What's he trying to achieve? Make it that much harder to attain. Is he on an epic journey to Mordor? Make them have to go the long route because the easy route just got blocked.

No animals were harmed in the experimenting of this chapter. My demon child did not, in fact, shave our cat and pour honey and feathers on it, that was just a delightfully twisted imagining from my dark mind.

Let's just throw some consequences out there. Here are a few ideas of consequences:

- Loss of relationship, friendship or lover
- More difficult, longer or complex journey
- Loss of power be it magical, authoritative or intangible
- Loss of or unable to retrieve information
- Loss of or unable to retrieve a needed item
- Loss of confidence, self-belief or other positive self-worth and value
- Loss of home, safety or food source

Representing the Conflict Realistically

Something to consider when creating your micro conflict is the need to ensure it's realistic. It's no good having two characters flop about on the page like suffocating fish. This shit needs to be deep and intense and meaningful.

Whichever characters are squabbling, the conflict should mean something to them both. Usually, writers worry about ensuring the conflict is meaningful to the hero and villain. But these micro conflicts extend to side characters and it's no less important. Which is why both characters involved need to be as invested in the fight as if losing will result in a public botty spanking, tomato throwing, hanging, drawing and quartering session.

But how do you create that level of argumentative intensity?

1. Specificity

Whatever the conflict, it needs to be specific. The more generalized a conflict, the harder it is to hook it to a particular person.

Global warming is worrying and potentially life threatening and while we should be united as a society to end it, we're not. Why? Because it's not specific enough. Yes, if the world heats up much more the ice caps will melt and we'll all die in a fit of mountain drowning chaos. But right now, in the here and now, it's too far away from too many of us. It's intangible and while we all have a vague understanding of the seriousness; it's not threatening enough of us individually for the majority of us to do anything about it.

Now, if you're writing an apocalyptic story where ice caps melt then of course it's going to be specific because I suspect two of your characters will be threatened by the same environmental disaster and they might have differing opinions on how to fix it. But that would apply to any human in that story world. It's still not specific enough. How about we get even more granular? Let's say character A is trying to win an award for environmental work through their plan to stop the ice caps melting, and character B is trying to get the same award abolished because their father died trying to win the award. Now that's specific.

In a contemporary romance, melting ice caps won't hit any conflict requirements because the two characters won't give a shriveled satan sphincter about penguins and polar bears. But they might fight over commitment to a relationship, or communication issues which are specific to their relationship. Make it specific and relevant.

2. Meaning

As well as being specific to each character, micro conflicts need to mean something to the characters involved. Take character B from the above example, they were trying to abolish the environmental award. But what if this character had a terrible relationship with their father and she didn't speak to him? Perhaps she never went to his funeral. Why would she care about the award? She'd be unlikely to try and take it down even if it had been the cause of his death. It would be meaningless to her and thus you lose the impetus of the conflict. Micro conflict as well as being specific to both characters, must mean something to them too.

3. Connect theme to micro conflict

If you want to sprinkle a little pizazz on your micro conflict, you can connect it to the theme. For example, in the movie *G.I. Jane*—and holy shit if you haven't seen this film what are you even doing with your life? It's one of my all-time fave girl power movies—the major theme was female power. Most of the conflict in the film was based on sexism and reducing Jane's female power. Master Chief—her trainer, boss, mentor and general thorn in her butt—constantly disrespected her, assumed she was weak and pitiful *because* she was a woman. They fought and fought and she had to earn every ounce of respect from him. In the ultimate girl power climax, Master Chief gets shot in the field and Jane picks his bleeding ass up and carries him out of the war zone to safety. She triumphed as a powerful woman and he had to respect her for it.

Okay let's look at some specific sources for creating micro conflict.

Family

One of the easiest methods to create micro conflict with side characters is through familial situations. Everyone knows how much siblings bicker. It's that love hate relationship that siblings thrive off. One minute they're playing with Lego and building world record breaking towers and the next minute they're seeing who can draw the most blood by smashing each other with the sharp end of a brick.

If you fancy a movie night, check out the Marvel movie *Thor*. Loki and Thor display hilarious sibling rivalry. Or how about Edmund and Lucy from *The Chronicles of Narnia,* lest we mention the cluster fuck of mortal sibling rivalry that is the Lannister family from *Game of Thrones*. And how about one of the oldest sibling rivalries, Cain and Abel from *Genesis* in *The Bible.*

One sure fire way to create conflict between your characters is to make their similar familial traits cozy up against each other or better yet, create juxtaposed traits to rub siblings up the wrong way.

Secrets and Lies

Ahh, secrets and lies, the sordid mysteries that serve to drive characters and readers alike bonkers. You can be assured though, that your readers will be turning those pages faster than a sugar deprived kid can shovel candy in their gob.

Secrets can be used in two ways to create conflict: having characters keep a secret or having them reveal it.

Secrets and lies are two sides of the same coin, rather than repeat myself with a secondary section on lies specifically, assume that you can replicate the principles of secrets across to lies—especially because the consequence of secrets is often having to lie. One follows the other follows the other, it's a big conflicty circle.

Keeping Secrets

Keeping secrets is the bread and butter of superhero status. Look at Clark Kent, desperate to keep his Superman identity secret. Or what about Batman and Bruce Wayne, or Peter Parker and Spiderman? Keeping their identity secret causes untold personal consequences between each superhero and their side character love interest.

What about other examples? A couple of other TV shows come to mind; *Prison Break's* entire premise is about secret keeping. Michael Scofield enters a prison (where his brother is being kept) with his body covered in tattoos. His aim is to bust his brother out of prison. A secret which he finds harder and harder to keep and ends up having to spill it to many of the inmates in order to have a team big enough to successfully bust out. Or, what about the much-loved show *Friends*. There were many secrets kept in that show, but one of my favorites was when Chandler and Monica were dating and trying to keep their affair secret.

To get a secret right on the page, you need to ensure it remains secret for as long as possible. What you absolutely don't want to do is allow your characters to realize there's a secret and then reveal it in the same chapter. You need to wait, allude to it, give half-truths and snippets, cause problems for the characters keeping the secret. Don't allow the truth to come out until much later in the plot. It's the "unknown" that drives readers through your pages wanting to unearth the dirty gossip.

Secret Consequence

Are you noticing a theme yet? With every conflict comes a consequence. Secrets between characters are a guaranteed method of creating conflict, but it's not guaranteed to sprinkle unicorn juice on your plot, that is, of course, unless you have a consequence for keeping that secret. Keeping the secret should be difficult for your characters. It should create chaos for their lives. Michael from *Prison Break* ends up having to work with his enemy in the prison who discovers his "break out" secret. It's a classic villain move though, to unearth a secret and then use it as blackmail.

Ask yourself: what are the consequences of your character keeping that secret? Here are some examples of consequences:

- Having to lie, or lie on top of lies
- Having to lie to loved ones or someone you promised not to lie to
- Struggling to keep multiple lies straight
- Killing for the secret
- Take an action that's against their moral fiber in order to protect the secret
- Battle with inner morals in order to keep the secret versus telling the truth
- Juggling guilt
- Getting ousted out of a group be it familial, social, or otherwise for keeping the secret

Spilling Secrets

Right, let's have a serious conversation now because while keeping the secret for most of the book is a must, so too is spilling the secret. You absolutely cannot open a secret as a story thread and then not close it by disclosing said secret to the reader. The only exception to that is if you're writing in a series and you need the secret to run through to another book —that should be clear to the reader though.

Secrets are made to be told—especially in stories. Think of them as a Chekov gun. The gun has to go off eventually and the secret needs to be told too. Refer back to the consequences section because there must be both a consequence for keeping the secret and a consequence for spilling it.

Listen, hero lovers, I know it's hard causing pain to your protagonist, but hear me roar because the best time to reveal a secret is when it will do the most damage. Got a secret your characters been keeping in order to keep a relationship going? Make sure it's revealed in the middle of a fight that will make or break their relationship. Been keeping a secret about a character who has a weapon you need? Cool, cool, reveal it just as the character was about to hand over the weapon.

Inhales

Oof

Too bad, no weapon for you Mrs. Hero. FIND ANOTHER WAY

Cackles

One other consideration is the personal or emotional change that might come from spilling a secret. While the outward consequence might be bad for relationships, the side character or protagonist revealing the secret may also feel a deep relief for giving up their secret. If this is the case, explore the juxtaposed interplay because it will serve to deepen characterization.

Shhh!

One other method to up the ante with secrets is to let your reader in on the secret without telling your protagonist.

How do you do this?

If you write in multiple points of view then this is surprisingly easy. You just switch out the point of view and reveal the secret from a side character's point of view.

However, if you only have one point of view or you're writing from first person point of view, then that is decidedly harder.

Where does that leave you? Foreshadowing is a fantastic way to tell the reader something without revealing it to the protagonist. For example, readers will pick up on comments from side characters that your protagonist doesn't. Pathetic fallacy and ominous weather, atmosphere changes and symbolism will all reveal information to the reader that your protagonist won't pick up on until they physically narrate the thought in prose.

All of these are essentially subtext, the information you're giving the reader between the lines. It's the only place the reader goes that the characters can't, which is why you can leave all the clues there.

Competition

Competition is a surefire way to create micro conflict. Whether it's protagonist versus side character or side character against side character, the conflict is in the competition itself. There can only be one winner in a competition, it's a fight to the death between characters to win. Just look at *The Hunger Games*. Of course, death stakes aren't compulsory, unless you're that way inclined, in which case, as you were. But the stakes *should* be high. Your characters should be willing to do things, *bad things, good things, naughty things, things that could get them arrested* in order to win. They need to want the prize, make sure it's both relevant and specific to all characters involved and that each of them has an equally valid motive for wanting the win.

Doubt

Side characters can be a fantastic way to create doubt in your protagonist. All it takes is a withheld piece of information, a scant look, some petty side eye, a whispered word to a third character, the intentional leaving out of the protagonist and all of a sudden, your hero is feeling paranoid.

Use this technique freely and regularly, your readers will love it.

Misunderstandings and Assumptions

Misunderstandings and assumptions are often but not always the consequence of doubt. They happen to be one of my favorite tools in the character bag because they're something lots of people do in real life.

Putting lies into your narrative prose rather than in dialogue is a great tactic for letting the reader into the secret truth of the protagonist's (or POV character's) emotions while hiding it from other characters. Tactics like this can lead to misunderstandings between characters and build tension. You can use this interruption technique to depict character realizations too.

And while we're talking about interruption, that is one of the key ways to create misunderstandings.

Let's say a side character love interest is trying to explain why they snogged the high school jock when they're supposed to be dating the protagonist. Instead of being able to explain themselves fully, the dialogue is interrupted either by another side character, by the protagonist themselves, or by an event. This will leave unexplained motives that will naturally lead the offended protagonist to draw incorrect conclusions.

How can you create misunderstandings? They can come in a multitude of forms. Here are a few ideas to get you going:

- A simple misunderstanding left unresolved at the end of dialogue between two characters
- A full-blown disagreement about a way forward,

about someone's behavior, about something said or
what a character did or didn't do
- A misunderstanding created by a lie
- Two characters engaging in dialogue but talking at
cross purposes
- Speaking in code that's misinterpreted
- Purposefully leaving out information that leads
another character to an incorrect assumption

8.3 MACRO CONFLICT

Okay word addicts, we're in the big leagues of conflict now. This type of conflict is the hardest to connect to side characters because it's world facing rather than person to person. For that reason, this section is shorter than the others as I believe the first two forms of conflict are far more important to your side characters.

However, we've established that the world can be a side character of sorts, let's roll with this and see where we get, shall we?

The Problem with Macro Conflict

Macro conflict is as outward facing as you can get. It's less about individual side characters and more about generational conflict. It's about war and law and seeds sown in the fabric of your worldbuilding.

This is khushty when creating wars in your world or battle-fields but not as good at drawing in individual side characters. It's too intangible and generalized.

Think back to Maslow's Hierarchy of Needs—macro

conflict typically hits the base levels, creating conflict from things like a lack of food, water, sleep, safety or security.

Macro conflict is a big bad wolf with no face—much like the corporate conglomerate organizations many of us used to (or still do) work for. You can't ever put your finger on the real villain because the organization itself is intangible and yet many of them do untold damage. This is the problem with macro conflict.

It's why it's important to build solid reasons for your side characters to engage with the macro conflict.

Let's use *The Hunger Games* as an example. The Capitol—the capital city of Katniss's world is the true villain. It stands for incredibly dark morals like segregation, death, control and sacrifice. But there is the connection to the theme. The book's theme is sacrifice, and The Capitol demands that each district sacrifice two children to its annual televised games: The Hunger Games. The games themselves create micro conflict in the battles between the children, but seeded in the games is the macro conflict that culminates in the final book—Katniss against The Capitol itself. And here is a couple of examples of where the macro conflict is made specific to the side characters and Katniss:

- The most generic connection is that the Capitol has tried to kill and control Katniss through the games and then after the games are over in her new life.
- Getting more specific, The Capitol controls how much food and resources her district receives access to. Meaning all the people she loves and cares about are at the whims of The Capitol. Including Peeta and Gale who are major side characters.
- And now most specifically, Katniss's sister (a side character) is threatened multiple times, starting with being picked during the Reaping (for the games) and

ultimately when she's then killed as a result of The
Capitol and the war.

If the macro conflict weren't connected to Katniss on these
multiple layers, her sister's death would be less meaningful.

Other forms of macro conflict include religion, power strug-
gles, societies or governments, generational or legacy issues,
historical events and established traditions, a loss of resource,
for example magic, that impacts all characters.

Connect Macro Conflict to the Theme

The last thing to say about macro conflict is that it's important to connect it to the theme of your story. It's no good having
a giant war in your story if it's not relevant to the overarching
message. In *The Hunger Games*, the theme is sacrifice, the
enemy demands child sacrifices, Katniss and her crew have to
make a million sacrifices to win, including the loss of loved
ones. The Capitol sacrifices its people in order to keep the
wealth for itself. The theme is tied in at every single level.

Questions to consider if you're including a macro conflict:

- How does the conflict impact your protagonist and
  side characters?
- Why do your side characters and protagonist care
  about this conflict?
- How is the macro conflict connected to your theme?
- How can you represent that connection through an
  event in your plot?
- Do you have side characters on both sides of the
  conflict?
- What would winning this macro conflict mean for
  the theme?

8.4 STORY CLIMAX

So, I'm sat here about to start writing this chapter and I'm like... wait one... "Story climax... Is that like the book's orgasm? Is every story ever about the big O? DO STORIES HAVE ORGASMS?" And here we shall stop the insights into my sordid mind.

This book is about side characters. But, unfortunately for them, the story climax is all about the hero. While your side characters can and probably should play a role in the story climax, it shouldn't be *the* role. They can't make the final villain-defeating blow, they cannot push the big red button, they cannot slay thy vicious demon. Why? Because that precious right is reserved for the protagonist. That's the case even in a heroine's journey. Soz. If a side character is playing a central role then you might wanna take yourself off to the side and ask whether your side character is really the main character. It sure as shit sounds like it.

Side characters of course have some involvement in the climax, but in a very protagonist centric way. It's the protagonist's conclusion—everything has been winding up to this moment, and unfortunately for our side-like friends, it's not about them. How can side characters be involved in the climax of your story then?

- They help, support, pressure, or influence your protagonist to move towards the story climax
- On the flip-side they hinder, distract, or pull your protagonist away from the story conclusion. In this instance, your side character is impacted negatively by your story climax and, most often, that's a result of the protagonist's choices
- They're not involved in the story climax, but represent it earlier in the book, be that symbolically, through a foreshadowing mechanism or otherwise
- They provide information, knowledge, or a key item which helps the protagonist reach their ultimate goal

That last one is key, really. All side characters are created to help the protagonist achieve their goal. In the goal-climax stakes the side characters should be focusing on helping the protagonist achieve that.

Side Character Conclusions

I don't want to rehash side character arcs, but it's worth mentioning here. Your side character arcs can be wrapped up more or less anywhere except in the story climax—though, of course, some of them may get wrapped up *as a result* of the climax. Want to wrap it up straight after? Cool. Want them to get beheaded in the final battle? Awesome, that works too. Just reserve the pinnacle of your story O for your protagonist and you're all good.

STEP 8 FIGHT TO THE DEATH SUMMARY

- Where we ate jelly and trifle, discovered books have orgasms, discussed big O's, fought, fought, fought, and realized I'm a bit more sordid than is polite.
- Creating conflict is as simple as **A + B = C**. Or in literary terms, **The existence of a goal + prevention of the goal being achieved = conflict.**
- There are three main types of conflict: macro, micro, and inner.
- Macro conflict is a larger scale, heavily outward-focused global war type of conflict.
- Micro conflict is the interpersonal, one-on-one fight, argument, or domestic between two characters.
- Inner conflict is the most inward facing conflict, a battle between oneself and... well, oneself.
- Conflict and side characters is a sliding scale. The less important the side character the less likely they are to create any conflict. Meaning, major characters are the ones who will wade into the fight with conflict cannons on their hips.
- Layering and balancing conflict—that is, ensuring

you have an element of each type of conflict in your
story—will create a more balanced novel overall.

- Examine Maslow's Hierarchy of Needs for ideas of
  the types of base conflicts you can use to feed your
  novel conflict.
- Time, and specifically added time pressure, will
  always be a nifty tool for upping the ante on your
  plot.
- Inner/emotional wounds are a common cause of
  inner conflict, so too are morals and values
  especially when they're put in direct conflict with
  each other. Another option is to have a physical
  representation of the wound.
- Consequences are the most important factor of any
  conflict you create. There must be a consequence be
  it good or bad to the conflict.
- Inner conflict can come from morals and values,
  politics, existential crises, love, self-image, beliefs,
  and love.
- Good sources of conflict for micro conflict are
  secrets and lies, both keeping a secret and spilling
  the beans. Other sources of micro conflict include
  doubt, competition, misunderstandings and
  assumptions, and family.
- To represent conflict realistically, make sure it's
  specific to both characters, that it means something
  to both of them, and it's connected to the book
  theme.
- The biggest problem with macro conflict is the fact
  it's intangible, meaning it's hard to connect it to your
  characters. Use layering to connect the characters to
  your conflict from generic through to specific
  connections.

Where possible, connect macro conflict to theme. Do this by asking yourself the following questions:

- How does the conflict impact your protagonist and side characters?
- Why do your side characters and protagonist care about this conflict?
- How is the macro conflict connected to your theme?
- How can you represent that connection in an event in your plot?
- Do you have side characters on both sides of the conflict?
- What would winning this macro conflict mean for the theme?

Questions to Think About

1. Identify stories in your genre that capture the three types of conflict.
2. Analyse the conflict in your favorite book. What is it about that conflict that grips you?

WANT MORE?

That's it, we've reached the end! There's just a couple more things to say before you go:

First of all, you can get your exclusive reusable side characters checklist, resource guide, and villains mini course by visiting: sachablack.co.uk/sidecharacters

Secondly, I hope you found this book helpful in your quest to craft better characters. If you liked the book and can spare a few minutes, I would be really grateful for a short review on the site from which you purchased the book. Reviews are invaluable to an author as it helps us gain visibility and provides the social proof we need to continue selling books.

Third, if you're looking for a supportive writing community, I run a Facebook group where I host a weekly accountability thread, writing prompts, and more. Join us here: facebook.com/groups/rebelauthors

From me to you, thank you for reading *8 Steps to Side Characters* and good luck with your writing journey.

AUTHOR'S NOTE

Some books won't die. This was one of them. My first book—
the one on villains—was vomited out. I had no expectations on
length, it was a spritely little thing, one of those miraculous
three-hour births jealous mothers blaspheme over.

The second book on heroes came out roughly the same
length. It was painful in its own way, what with being the
second book I had to fight my own psychological bullshit to
push that baby over the line.

The third book on prose, however, was a vicious little
fucker. It came out kicking and screaming, it exploded from the
start, replicating like a virus on steroids. I knew from the outset
it was going to be a beast.

But this book... Ohhh, this one was more than mischievous,
it was an insidious little bastard. Side characters crept up on
me, adding sections and chapters, shoving interesting articles
or books in my way so that I had no choice but to continue writing. This "little" book on side characters that I was going to
"whip out"—you naive fool—went from my predicted 40,000
words to almost 80,000 at its peak. I feel like I went through
several stages of grief while writing it, anger and pure rage,

denial, evil eyeing my laptop. On and on it went, until finally, finally I got the book done and laid quietly on my office floor weeping from the sheer relief of it.

Writing books is amazing, and exhausting but the most fun job a girl could ask for. I love that each book creates its own personality as it's written. Watch out for this one, she bites... but only on Tuesdays, and only if you're naughty.

Sacha Black
May, 2021.

ACKNOWLEDGMENTS

I wrote this book over the course of the pandemic, a time when many found their creativity waning or struggling. I genuinely don't think I could have written it without my daily sprint buddies: Dan Willcocks, Katlyn Duncan, and Crys Cain. You guys keep me going, call me out on my bullshit and antagonize my inner competition... I mean "encourage" her... you *encourage* my competition. It is in times of dire difficulties that friends become more important than ever, and I thank you. Alongside those morning sprints, I regularly use Becca Syme's "The Office" which allows me to quietly get on but gives me friendly faces to see every day.

Thank you to my writing friends, Helen J, Suzie, Helen S, and Jenna, each of you keeping a different piece of my soul sane!

My wife, of course, who puts up with her authorly-neurotic spouse and encourages me to follow the dream. To my son, who all of this is for, whether you want to be a YouTuber, an astronaut, or a vet, I hope that I've shown you anything is possible if you study hard, work hard, and go big or go home. World domination, son, that's what you aim for.

Thank you to the authors who let me quote their knowledge and wisdom, specifically Jeff Elkins and Angeline Trevena.

To my Rebel Author Facebook Group, thank you for being so supportive, engaging, and downright devious, you make weekly accountability so much fun and I really appreciate all of your input and answering of my incessant questions.

My patrons:

Orna, Icy, Tom, Christine, Matt, Daisy, Patrick, Shae, Sarah, Aime, Alison, Arriane, Holly, Julia, Yanni, Angela, Faye, Katlyn, Daniel, Carey, Steven, Bair, Jackie, Cari, Jay, Rae, Denise, William, Mary, Stacy, Renee, Heather, Cindy, Harley, Juneta, Emma, Jeff, Victoria, Marcus, Janelle, Crys, Cassie, Naomi, Helen, Nicole, Martina, Jackson, Stanley, Harry, Scott, Giannin, Jasmine, Jen, Noelle, Nathan, Moninder, Heather, Kate, Lynne, Tauna, Jennifer, Shelly, Stephanie, S.W., Laura, Matty, Lucie, Eden, Moninder.

Thank you for your continued support; you make me feel like what I do matters, and it means more than words can express.

And to you, dear reader, thank you for investing your time in this book. I hope that you've learned something, and it helps you along your journey to your writing dreams.

ALSO BY SACHA BLACK

The Better Writers Series

Sacha has a range of books for writers. If you want to improve your villains, your heroes or your prose, she's got you covered.

To improve your villains:

13 Steps to Evil: How to Craft a Superbad Villain

13 Steps to Evil: How to Craft a Superbad Villain Workbook

To improve your heroes:

10 Steps to Hero: How to Craft a Kickass Protagonist

10 Steps To Hero - How To Craft A Kickass Protagonist Workbook

 To improve your prose:

The Anatomy of Prose: 12 Steps to Sensational Sentences

The Anatomy of Prose: 12 Steps to Sensational Sentences Workbook

The 9 Things Series with J Thorn:

9 Things Career Authors Don't Do: Personal Finance

9 Things Career Authors Don't Do: Rebel Mindset

ABOUT THE AUTHOR

Sacha Black is a bestselling and competition winning author, rebel podcaster, speaker and casual rule breaker. She has five obsessions; words, expensive shoes, conspiracy theories, self-improvement, and breaking the rules. She also has the mind of a perpetual sixteen-year-old, only with slightly less drama and slightly more bills.

Sacha writes books about people with magical powers and other books about the art of writing. She lives in Cambridgeshire, England, with her wife and genius, giant of a son.

When she's not writing, she can be found laughing inappropriately loud, blogging, sniffing musty old books, fangirling film and TV soundtracks, or thinking up new ways to break the rules.

sachablack.co.uk/newsletter
www.sachablack.co.uk
sachablack@sachablack.co.uk

Image Credit @Lastmanphotography

instagram.com/sachablackauthor
bookbub.com/authors/sacha-black
facebook.com/sachablackauthor
twitter.com/sacha_black
amazon.com/author/sachablack